History of Money and Usury in America

By Daniel S. Krynicki

Independent History and Research
Box 849
Coeur d'Alene, Idaho 83816

www.revisionisthistory.org

Printed in the United States of America

History of Money and Usury in America
Part I
"A Christian Nation?"

By Daniel S. Krynicki
April 17, 2014

Introduction

Those who decide to read an essay such as this either suspect or know we are being taken for a ride, laboring for little or no return by a band of international criminals through our elected officials and educators. That they are able to keep the majority of people in the dark as to how they do this should give us plenty of incentive to learn some economics terminology. As a rule, this is a vapid study ; but by condensing the fundamentals of money creation, the entire subject can become understandable to anyone.

It is possible to drive the moneychangers out of the temple now ; but which monetary system would replace theirs once they are removed? Do we have a clear enough vision which would enable us to institute an alternative system that will work for the common good? Attempts have been made to throw the moneychangers out of the temple several times in American history ; but even the best intentions were unobtainable without first considering that usury is at the root of their power ; and consequently the struggle has always ended with the private money creators winning. To win, it will also be necessary to be as strong-willed as Andrew Jackson was during the 'Bank Wars' of the 1830s when he vetoed legislation to renew the Second Bank of the United States. The assassination attempt on his life was thwarted. But two other presidents, whose administrations denied the bankers their usury by paying for public dues with Treasury Department issued legal tender notes, did not survive. So this battle with bankers over usury has always turned sanguinary. Educating a critical mass of the population will be a necessary component in this conflict ; so we must first learn precisely how this created money is released into the currency stream before entering the struggle to implement the only correct cure.

Money and Usury

Most money is created as interest bearing debt by banks and has been for well over three hundred years. When the Federal *1666* Reserve Act was passed giving ownership of a new banking institution known as the Federal Reserve to a privately owned cartel of international bankers, Congress transferred its constitutional authority to create our money to this privately owned corporation. Proof that this authority belongs to Congress is presented further on in this paper.

Several forms of money in use are as follows:

Coins are minted by the United States government. Our government pays no interest to anyone for Coins. They are stamped and dated at various US Mint locations and released into the currency stream at authorized Fed member banks, including credit unions that are also licensed to operate as banking functionaries. Coins make up an insignificant amount of the money supply; and they are legal tender for all debts, public and private. [1]

Paper currency that are presently known as Federal

Reserve Notes is also legal tender. Paper currency has been around since Colonial times in America. The Chinese printed paper currency during the 11th century. Bank notes as paper currency were common during mid 19th century America. They were redeemable for specie (gold coin) at private banks. At various other times public paper currency has circulated under different names. Most of these were legal tender.

Were!

Gold backed paper currency was in use in America prior to and at the beginning of the Federal Reserve until 1933 when FDR ended the ability of individual Americans to demand gold (specie) in return for their paper currency.

But with all these technical distinctions that the various forms of money have taken on, it is imperative to understand that all of them constitute the means by which people are able to rid themselves of a primitive barter system. [2]

There is nothing inherently evil in using money as a medium of exchange ; but the way in which most money is first created as interest bearing debt guarantees that all people will continue to remain under high finance's debt oppression. An elite cartel in high finance has complete control of this process. Money, to these parasites, has consequently become a **fungible** rather than what it simply should be: a **medium of exchange**. We shall explore this line of reasoning further in this essay.

Gold

The purveyors of gold backed money (formerly called gold brokers [3]) are still with us. Their hue and cry is forever against the use of unbacked paper currency. They call it **fiat money**. [4] One web site where anyone can read their gold propaganda is at: < www.lewrockwell.com >. Active educators and elected officials involved in this web site should be well known by all. Two of them are Gary North and Ron Paul. Fiat money to these two is a derogatory term. We should always be alert to their advertising devices. North's twisting of the plain intent on usury that the Bible teaches leads unaware Christians into believing false paradigms. If the foundations for all his teaching are fundamentally flawed through misinterpretation of the Christian Bible, then his version of Christian economics is at best spurious. Additionally, there are quite a few expert opinions that refute the gold advocates squarely on this issue. Mr. North was also quite obtuse in a hatchet job he did on economist Gertrude Coogan, so we should expect nothing reliable from him about anything. Later on much more will be presented herein showing that Ms. Coogan's insight was superior to North's grasp of Christian economics.

As an example, a recent email to my inbox from the crowd North aligns himself with over at the Daily Bell declared, "Gold is the only Constitutional money". Do they fool 90% of the population with statements like this? They most likely do. But this clause [5] in the Constitution was placed there so that states would be allowed to issue only gold as currency in their respective states. The Continental Congress and the First Bank of the United were emitting 'Bills of Credit' as loans of paper currency (mostly legal tender) [6] at interest to the general population during America's formative years. So this gold clause in the Constitution was only added to reserve the authority to create paper money as legal tender for Congress. Every little clause taken out of context that ignores the facts of history can produce enough disinformation to keep the people ignorant of the elements of truth contained in every story. It behooves us to learn the whole truth about money creation in America because this knowledge only will illuminate the way to overcome the anglers and connivers of high finance.

Fiat Money and Bank Credit

Fiat money is money that derives its value from government regulation or law (From Wikipedia). [4] The Colonial American governments emitted fiat paper money known as 'Bills of Credit'. It was issued primarily as loans at interest to the general population. During the Civil War, the US government issued two types of fiat paper currency notes to pay Union troops and other expenditures needed to prosecute the war [7]. The gold advocates referred to them as 'Greenbacks' and claim that nothing backed them. We will show herein that their disdain for fiat money is not justified. Any legal tender created by edict (or fiat if you will) is always backed by collateral, that is, by the people with their assets and labor. Furthermore, when a government emits this fiat money, as payment directly in return for labor and infrastructure that is needed in funding the costs of government, that labor and infrastructure actually give the created money real value. Something useful has been received in return for the money that was created. We can call this money "credit" upon which no interest has to be paid and it remains in circulation as 'purchasing power' by whomever it was paid to. This credit money will also be legal tender even if it only appears on our radar in an account balance as cyberspace digits. It is the sort that Thomas Edison identified in his famous Mussel Shoals editorial letter from the 1920s [8]. In this type of credit a government creates legal tender notes, fiat money, Greenbacks or 'bills of credit', whatever the snide usurers decide to call them, to pay directly for infrastructure projects without borrowing and without paying interest to anyone and without paying back principal to anyone.

Article 1 Section 8 Line 5 of the Constitution explicitly authorizes Congress to do this. But instead of creating money in this way, Congress and an idiot President passed the Federal Reserve Act on December 23, 1913 giving this authority to create our money over to a cartel of international bankers. Elected officials in our national government therefore do not have either the intelligence or the wit to issue the money our nation needs to conduct its business. And instead of lending, usury free to its own citizens, of this money that it has the authority to create, it

6

borrows from these international criminal cartels almost everything that enters our currency stream.

Presently, loaning of credit at interest by private banks does not depend on work performed. This is **Bank Credit**. **[9]** It is based on a borrower's ability to pay along with an asset that is offered by the borrower as collateral. These are two necessary components in the terms of any loan ; and the loan process involves a contract spelling out terms with signatures. We can call this bank credit "money" because it actually acts as money in our present system. Credit cards fall under this definition. All in all, it comprises about 90% to 97% of our circulating money supply. Bank credit, therefore, works very well as money while in the currency stream. It is suitable for use as money because 90% of the business world accepts it as payment for their products or services. Technically, though, it does not fall under the definition of legal tender. There is no gold or any other commodity to purportedly back it, so it greatly resembles fiat money. But when push comes to shove all money allowed into the currency stream legally is fiat money. The gold advocates miss the whole point. Even their purportedly 'gold backed money' is also fiat. That is, it is nothing but paper or linen with ink, or cyberspace ledger entries upon which they expect to collect usury.

Consider the following: Money must have a beginning ; that is, it must be created before it can circulate. When it is created as direct payment for any services performed, it has value in the service performed, or in the finished product that was purchased. If the government paid for the building of a bridge over a waterway out of created fiat money, the bridge itself would indeed be an equity that is testament to the value of the money. In this way money would actually be created and then given in return for the labor and materials needed to pay for something. Now the money that paid for the bridge remains in circulation unless or until it is taxed out of existence. So while this money remains in circulation, it still has value. If money is borrowed at interest from private money creators to pay for the bridge, the cost of the bridge may double, triple or possibly go even higher depending upon both the term of the loan and the interest rate (see centerfold on pages 28, 29). And when the principal of the bridge loan is paid back to a private lender, it vanishes from the currency stream. At that point the money disappears and therefore no longer has any value.

Ordinary interest, which we call usury, is not paid to anyone on money that would get issued by a National Credit Agency (NCA). It is considered as public money. Later on herein, we will learn how our American government and Colonial governments created money in this way at various times in the past.

Public money is a very reasonable concept in that all money that enters the currency stream affects the public weal. Too much money in the currency stream chasing after goods and services may cause price inflation. This bureaucracy would therefore also be charged with regulating the money supply so that just the right amount of money remains in circulation. Too little money in the currency stream would cause commercial activity to slow down. Too much money in the currency stream may cause price inflation.

Since this National Credit Agency issues money into the currency stream out of the labor of government employees, administration expenses and infrastructure projects, it is no stretch of the imagination to visualize that it can also issue loans to all without charging usury or even fees. In this way 'Promote the General Welfare' will be the Preamble mandate that would at last be fulfilled. The costs involved in administration of an NCA that lends usury free are paid for directly out of the people's credit in the same way as the direct funding of government is done. If we can visualize this so easily, we can also determine that if there is still not an adequate money supply for commercial activity, then why not fund directly in this way all public service jobs that

8

would include wages and pensions for police, fire and paramedic ambulance services. We can eliminate homestead property taxes, gasoline taxes, and estate taxes. We can eliminate all taxes except one that would be necessary to keep the money supply and Gross Domestic Product balanced. This tax, however, must not be an income tax. The only fair tax is one that does not kick in until after individuals reach a cost of living threshold. It would be a tax on increase ; and therefore it would be in compliance the Mosaic Law requirements.

Public or Private NCA – What shall it be?

Interest is normally always paid on privately created money whether purportedly gold backed or simply collateral backed. The principal of this kind of money vanishes from existence as it is paid back to the lender. But the interest the lender acquires as the loan is paid back does not vanish. The lender gets to keep it as profit. We therefore understand why honest economists explain that the modern moneylending process is fundamentally deflationary. It is because more money leaves the currency stream as a loan is retired than was created at the signing of a loan. Conversely, NCA money creations that are paid directly into government operations are never paid back to anyone. Once this direct funding money is created and pays for labor and/or materials, it remains in circulation. It therefore has something that gives it value: namely, a system of laws along with the means to enforce them. That something behind it may also be a bridge as well as the operations of a criminal justice system. And the created money can operate as a medium of exchange without the hindrance of making an object of idol worship out of it. Notice also that in such a system critical government operations like police and criminal justice will always be **fully funded**. In this way our government, acting of, for and by the people, creates its own permanent money supply.

Howard Benjamin Rand, LL.B.

To aid our analysis on monetary matters we will now reference the Christian Bible. This is a book in which money matters were written about as far back as three and a half millennia ago. Two modern scholars claim our Christian Bible has prohibited usury in money lending dating back that far. Each has or had a different specialty area in learning. So we will begin here with the late Howard B. Rand as one of the most complete exegetes we have been able to observe in our lifetimes.

Mr. Rand, who passed away in 1991 at the age of 104, had an LL.B. degree. He passed the bar in Maine in 1912 and in Massachusetts in 1913. He was thus licensed to practice law in two states. He practiced law and owned a construction company until 1928 when he became the National Commissioner of the Anglo-Saxon Federation of America. There should be no need to enumerate all of his subsequent accomplishments and books. Two books, though, are of special interest to those of us who have lately focused our attention on national monetary matters. Howard Rand's books that address this in no uncertain terms are his *Digest of Divine Law* and *Study in Revelation*. (Destiny Publishers)

Mr. Rand wrote perhaps 20 to 30 books along with essays too numerous to count in analysis of the Scriptures. Also, other indicators from his writings show that he searched out not just the Scriptures, but also the historical records found in modern academia. He did not provide us with too much in the way of details about his reasoning on interpretation of the two ancient Biblical languages. He merely rendered his opinions on key doctrinal points in landmark studies, such as the two aforementioned books. We must also take notice of the latter because there is some related information in it about our present commercial system he identifies as *"The Babylonian methods of commerce"*. What he wrote was, no doubt, the result of painstaking research by including many reputable Bible translations as well as scrutinizing very carefully the ancient dialects for himself.

So here is Mr. Rand about usury in his ***Digest of Divine Law*** from page 94:

*"In these three important laws a perfect monetary system based upon the value of goods, services and the increase of our national wealth **with the outlawing of usury** and the institution of a system of taxation which is not confiscatory of property, the foundation will have been laid for an economic structure which in operation will be par excellent. Nothing that the socialists can conceive nor the Communists desire can be compared to the institution of the God-given system which will out-capital capitalism in that all men will become capitalists and 'sit every man under his vine and under his fig tree; and none shall make them afraid; for the mouth of the Lord of hosts hath spoken it.'   In this statement is the*

Howard B. Rand, LL.B.

assurance of food and drink, to replace the fear and want which is ever present with men under the present economy."

Careful reading of Leviticus chapter 25 should lead readers to understand that, with certainty, domestic usury was prohibited in ancient Israel. Today, we not only have oppressive taxation with all manner of taxes, including income, estate and homestead property taxes ; we also have the widespread practice of usury, not just internationally, but nationally as well. The fact is, though, that Mr. Rand held his opinion of **"with the outlawing of usury"** from a complete analysis of all the related Scriptures. **[10]** We should expect he did exhaustive analysis of the ancient Chaldee words ger and nokri in the contexts they are found in Leviticus and Deuteronomy. But the commandments of Jesus have been expanded now in the New Testament to include all nations in which every man is now our brother. We are now to 'go into all the world and preach the gospel to every creature'. If Israel was commissioned to expand and fill the earth, it was done so that salvation and the kingdom of God will be preached to all. So who are we to dispute the words that Luke reported Jesus spoke in Luke 6:35, "Lend, asking for nothing in return"? All those who seek to identify themselves as adherents of the Christian faith are also enjoined to keep the commandments of Jesus. Else, how could they claim they love Jesus?

If we are not to be found negligent in teaching the Kingdom evangel, we need to first humble ourselves from the pride of being the elect, the chosen of God and begin teaching the entire gospel story as servants, not as masters. We should note here that Mr. Rand, in one of his booklets, identifies Israel as "The Servant People" ; he considers that the heirs of promise bear the burden of expanding Christ's kingdom. With identity comes responsibility. This will include the prohibition of all usury in simple loan contracts. It also means nationally - making money nothing more than a medium of exchange. Remember, the Lord resists the "proud". Who is there among us prideful enough to countermand a direct order from the King of the kingdom?

12

Included here also are excerpts from **_Study in Revelation_** so that those who have not had the opportunity to study Rand can read for themselves what an honest scholar has written about our present monetary system.

From Pages 278, 279:
"Come out of Her My People:
"The call now goes forth for God's people to leave the system 'that ye be not partakers of her sins, and that ye receive not of her plagues.'

"This call indicates that Israel is in the system and carrying on her commercial activities in conformity with the requirements of Babylon. As the time of judgment approaches God calls his people to leave the system.

"It would be unjust to call upon Israel to leave the Babylonian methods of commerce if there were not another system already waiting Israel's adoption in this time of emergency. Now there is such a system and it was given to His people at Mount Sinai. Israel departed from its observance and, in the adoption of the methods of Babylon, acquired the economic evils of that heathen system. Accompanying this call for Israel to leave the Babylonian system of economics is the way they are to go, now being pointed out through the proclamation of the Kingdom message. Attention is being called to their God-given laws of administration and His perfect system of economics which is par excellence. While Israel continues under Babylonian methods she is *partaking of her sins, and receiving of her plagues.*

"The Sins Of Babylon:

"For her sins have reached unto heaven, and God hath remembered her iniquities. Reward her even as she rewarded you, and double unto her double according to her works: in the cup which she hath filled fill to her double.

"This sentence is pronounced in accord with the Israel law of judgment in matters of economic justice. This again confirms the fact that in this chapter John is witnessing the judgment upon the economic and not the ecclesiastical phase of Babylonian manifestation.

"The present economic system has been unjust, oppressive and has taken from God's people the fruit of their labors. It is judged a usurper and thief. The law says, 'For all manner of trespass, whether it be for ox, for ass, for sheep, for raiment, or for any manner of lost thing, which another challenges to be his, the cause of both parties shall come before the judges; and whom the judges shall condemn, he shall pay double unto his neighbor. (Ex. 22:9.)"

Thus Rand rendered his opinion not only as a Bible scholar but also as a legal analyst that all usury is now outlawed.

14

Michael Hoffman

But Rand was only one witness. We can only establish matters by evidence obtained from at least two or three witnesses. In this matter of usury there are many more additional witnesses besides Rand, all laid out in proper order by historian Michael Hoffman in his ***Usury in Christendom: The Mortal Sin That Was and Now is Not***. Mr. Hoffman is the second witness through his indefatigable searches of historical data that pertain to usury in Christendom. Every item of history (and there are many) in his book is testament to the fact that usury is not and never was allowed to be practiced by anyone aspiring to be included in God's kingdom, especially with the advent of the New and Everlasting Covenant. Synod after synod, the Council at Nice, numerous Lateran Councils, Psalms 15:1-5, and the ten volumes of the Ante-Nicene Fathers all testify to this fact. For fourteen plus centuries subsequent to the sub-Apostolic period, this proscription against usury was in effect. Has God changed His mind about usury? Men, who have itching ears have contorted and twisted with escape clauses that which the Scriptures plainly state because of their love of money and their love of the Babylonian commerce. One Old Testament allowance of usury, through misinterpretation and misappropriation, has been used by modern so-called interpreters of the Bible to nullify the international injunctions spoken of with Christ's own mouth. Isn't it enough to accept Christ's plainly stated words, "Lend, asking for nothing in return"? Christ's mission indeed was to bring the kingdom of God to men on earth, the whole earth. It was for this very same purpose He appeared to Moses at Mt. Sinai, to establish the kingdom of God on earth with righteous legal and financial systems as an example for that day when He ushers in His everlasting kingdom visibly. Only in the New Testament He expounded more perfectly the parameters with which His servants should operate in His service from that point in time forward. The kingdom evangel was now extended to the uttermost parts of the earth; whosoever will is now included to be eligible for kingdom citizenship; and all usury on loans of money is now outlawed.

Revisionist historian Michael Hoffman

Jesus Christ provided for us in the New Testament His unequivocal approbation of virtually all of the Old Testament. [11] By telling us that a greater than Solomon stood among them, He acknowledged that Solomon's writings were inspired. He also quoted from the Psalms, the Law and the Prophets, and therefore acknowledged all of them as inspired by God. So anyone, who has it in mind to innovate legal and monetary civil systems beyond that which the Christian Bible has already revealed, is treading dangerous waters.

In addition to Rand's and Hoffman's books there are four additional books in support of this proof that usury in the creation of money is the real reason our American founding documents are an abysmal failure at delivering their intended results. Though none of these four actually identify usury as the reason for this failure, yet if the reader honestly assesses all the facts, this conclusion will become unavoidable:

1. Mark Valeri out of Princeton University Press published a landmark study in 2010 with the title *Heavenly Merchandize:*

How Religion Shaped Commerce in Puritan America. Hoffman used this book for much of his source material on Puritan America in early New England. This book is now available in states with library cooperatives that have check out privileges to library cardholders. One no longer has to travel long distances to a far away university library in order to check it out. It can be requested for delivery to a local library at no charge and then kept at home to study for several weeks. Libraries also normally offer extensions of time on checkouts for further study. Of course, Mr. Hoffman's section on early Puritan America is only one small part of his book covering history for the past three thousand five hundred years.

The second, third and fourth documents mentioned next are all available on line. Two were free downloads about a year ago. They are in order as follows:

2.   <   http://books.google.com/books/about/Financial_Histor y_of_the_United_States.html?id=l3oaAAAAMAAJ > PDF - This *Financial History of the United States* was published in 1915 by a PH.D. MIT professor named Davis Rich Dewey.   This is a Google Books free download. Doing a Google search for this title will disclose that there are actually more than one free downloads in PDF for this book. [6] If it is no longer available as a download, it is nevertheless available for free viewing on line. From the on line viewing, a reader should be able to save pages into a document file as a PNG or at least be able to print pages.

3.   < http://etext.lib.virginia.edu/users/brock/webdoc6.html > - This one is Benjamin Franklin's *A Modest Enquiry into the Nature and Necessity of a Paper-Currency*. This web page is not in PDF. It must be copied and pasted from the web page to some text editor capable of rich text format. BFWW

4. < https://archive.org/details/MoneyCreators > PDF This book from 1935, ***Money Creators***, was written by a lady who held a master's degree in economics and finance from Northwestern University. She also worked at a securities company for eight years. Her name was Gertrude Coogan. In her book she exposed the United States Federal Reserve System for what it is: a scam. [12] But right after the passage cited in endnote twelve, she disclosed her ignorance of sound Christian doctrine that explicitly prohibits the charging of interest on simple loans. Though she was brilliant in her presentation on money creation and the way in which we should do this without usury at the national level, she missed the obvious truth that if money can be created by a national bureaucracy to pay for the costs of government, that bureaucracy can also create credit to lend usury free, perhaps even fee free, especially to its own citizens.

Mutuum and Mutual Risk Contract

Let us consider what a simple loan is, a ***mutuum***. It is a simple loan of a fungible such as money (capital) which the debtor repays as the exact sum loaned (from Hoffman [***Usury in Christendom***] page 394). Notice from this definition of *mutuum*, this is necessarily capital that already exists. In today's monetary system, credit is therefore not a fungible because lenders create new money every time a loan transaction is signed. From the second century AD onward, until 1515 AD the catholic Church of Jesus Christ, from all of the various synods, councils and all of the writings of the Apostolic Fathers, the charging of interest on the *mutuum* loan was prohibited. The penalty for laity doing this was excommunication by a church that then had powerful influence in civic affairs. This proscription against usury was in effect even when the money lent already existed, as in the

18

mutuum. But now the people, through ignorance, have given privately owned banks the authority to issue loans (or credit) out of money that doesn't even exist. This is **bank credit that enters the currency stream and it has deflationary effects on the money supply**. As money, it is not truly a fungible because it doesn't exist before a loan is issued ; and it exists no more after it is paid back. For all who do some useful service or labor for their earnings, their money is a fungible under today's usurious monetary system. But for all those who create money, it is not a fungible ; it is only a tool. It is a tool indeed that only bankers have accessibility to manipulate. Where did it come from? Where did it go if it didn't exist to begin with? Presto, they didn't have the money to lend, but they collect usury on it anyway. It's like magic. *not like, it is magic!*

There is also such a thing as a *contract of mutual risk*. These are easily identifiable today as shareholders, partnerships and joint business ventures. In these transactions capital normally used in the agreement is usually capital that already exists.

Ownership in this type of business is normally determined proportionally by the ratio of capital invested. For businesses that are considered legitimate, this ratio of ownership is easily learned from consulting Yahoo or Google Finance. Any corporation listed at one of the public trading exchanges has shareholder information on display there. For instance, a military defense contractor/manufacturer will have on display there what percentage of shares are held by institutional and fund sources. Institutional is short for international bankers, and thus perhaps overlooked by most who read it. And funds may very well be owned primarily by banking families, thus giving the oligarchs controlling interest anyway. So even with the funds, full disclosure of the facts is lacking. We can only wonder how sly they have been since 1999 with the passage of the Financial Services Modernization Act dismantling FDR's Glass-Steagall.

At any rate, beginning in 2008, institutional and fund

ownership has markedly declined in US corporations. In 2006 Washington Group International was 97% owned by banking institutions and funds. At the same time DTE Energy Company in southeastern Michigan was 66% owned by banking institutions and funds. These controlling interest ratios are down considerably today as the result of offshoring our manufacturing sector. DTE Energy's megawatt load has been cut in half since the last recession began due to manufacturing facilities closing. Forty years of offshoring manufacturing infrastructure has taken its toll ; and now it's worse since 2009 when credit to businesses was curtailed. It appears that our princes of industry care not if their own nation prospers. And in the case of WGI, our presence in both Afghanistan and Iraq is almost over.

Another complication across the past one hundred years is found in the formation of holding or shell corporations. Since banking institutions have the authority to create new money, they then use this new money for lending to these holding companies and/or shell corporations which in turn obtain majority ownership in military defense contractors/manufacturers and any corporation they deem will be profitable. Senator Carl Levin of Michigan recently introduced legislation that would prohibit the formation of anonymously owned corporations in the United States. **[13]** Criminals have in recent years been using this method of escaping the scrutiny of law enforcement. How long of course have banking institutions been allowed to do this? Or more important, did the criminals learn of this trick from lawyers who worked for bankers? Finally, will any escape clauses be introduced into the legislation that would exempt banking institutions and funds from complying with the law that is finally passed?

These are the "Rules of Acquisition" Quark talked about on Deep Space Nine, "War is good for profits; Peace is good for profits." Don't think this is a joke. Proof for all this is at our fingertips today on the internet.

Even with all of this in plain sight, very few realize the

* not good

only way we can end the international bankers' hegemony requires a three part solution: first, the power to create our money must be taken away from institutionalized, privately owned banks and returned to the people through the aegis of legitimate government ; the second part of this solution is to end once and for all time the practice of usury in moneylending on simple loan contracts ; and the third part of this solution is to take any ownership rights internationalists have in domestic corporations. A proportionate share of ownership in domestic corporations should be vested in citizen employees. Employees also sacrifice of their time daily. They should therefore be partakers of a proportionate share of dividends that are created through the mutual risk contract. Dual loyalists must not be allowed to have ownership in domestic corporations or hold public office. This removing the shackles international finance has on us will require implementation of all three steps. Anything short of this will most likely fail.

In both of these types of contracts, *mutuum* or **contract of mutual risk**, the historical reality was that the money already existed at the signing of the contract.

The CPAs and lawyers, though, take definitions from ages past, then contort and twist intended meanings and thus use them for the modern way in which money is created. They actually consider that newly created money in a loan contract today is actually lending a fungible good. (**Fungibility** is the property of a good or a commodity whose individual units are capable of mutual substitution, such as sweet crude oil, shares in a company, bonds, precious metals, currencies, or pistachios - from http://en.wikipedia.org/wiki/Fungible). With this as a definition, a lender must give up something he possesses, something real, something that is at risk in addition to the collateral a borrower has at risk. This money bankers create in the loan contract is indeed real in their minds. But what happens after the borrower has paid back principal plus interest across a twenty-year period.

Let us project that the international bankers who are in control of the economy decide to curtail credit at a point in time to put the brakes on economic activity. They do this by not lending front capital to the business community, especially to smaller businesses that are not part of their circle of holding companies or shell corporations. These businesses then have no money to make payroll or purchase materials in the beginning of the year as is customary with their fiscal practices. In 2009 this is precisely what happened when millions of skilled laborers were laid off. Did the bankers who engineered this recession care one whit that a family which paid on their mortgage for twenty years wound up losing their homestead property? On a $100,000 5% mortgage they would, by this time, have already have paid $128,000 to the lender along with any up front mortgage fees and points. When the property occupant is uprooted from his home by eviction after foreclosure proceedings, does the mortgagor or tax assessor consider any of this? Definitely not! But mortgagors do get an income tax break for the necessity to run the homestead through their system as additional costs. Does the reader see anything wrong with this picture? This could only be the result from lawyers and bankers stretching the definition of fungible to mean something it doesn't.

It isn't written anywhere in the Bible that we are not allowed to create and use our own money for commerce. But it did, in a number of places, at first restrict our use of usury. However, in the new an everlasting covenant a commandment was issued prohibiting usury in all moneylending. Domestically it was prohibited in the Mosaic Law. It was even not allowable to charge interest on loans to aliens who lived peaceably within ancient Israel's borders and who kept God's everlasting moral laws. Finally in the New Testament Jesus told us that we must lend, asking for nothing in return. This is quite a straightforward statement, but if implemented domestically, it would simply be in compliance with the Law of Moses as it was required in ancient

Israel. So, Jesus's statement in Luke 6:35 was nothing new under the sun. I don't see any escape clauses freeing us from the burden of this responsibility. If as Howard Rand recounted from Exodus 22:9, the law requires of violators *"for all manner of trespass"* that double be repaid, then woe are the American corporations that have raped, pillaged and plundered so many other nations through their usury lending and slave labor tactics used both abroad and domestically. But what also of the millions and millions of violent premature deaths and horrific suffering that they are also responsible for? I ask the Lord at His judgment seat to have mercy on me and my family, for we did not approve of their monetary policies nor did we approve of going to war so they could expect returns on their military/industrial blood money.

If readers have not yet grasped the seriousness of this study on kingdom evangel, then it is recommended here and now that they consider the following New Testament passages:

Luke 6:35 "Lend, asking for nothing in return."

Matthew 7:14 "Straight is the gate, narrow is the way that leads to life, and few there be who find it."

Luke 11:23 "He that is not with me is against me: and he that gathereth not with me scattereth."

Matthew 13:30 "Let both grow together until the harvest: and in the time of harvest I will say to the reapers, Gather ye together first the tares, and bind them in bundles to burn them: but gather the wheat into my barn."

Luke 19:27 "But those mine enemies, which would not that I should reign over them, bring hither, and slay them before me."

Of course, there are those who through the ignorance of not reading the Scriptures, have erred in their tacit compliance with the world's ways. They have blindly trusted leaders and pastors who have itching ears, who are supposed to be experts at teaching Christian doctrine, but who are really followers of predecessors that have abandoned completely sound New Testament doctrine. Jesus said simply, "If you love me keep my commandments". Well the top one given above is and has been summarily ignored by our national leadership since before this nation was born in 1776. So how can this be a Christian nation?

American History and the Constitution

There has been much disinformation circulating for some time now on the internet concerning American History. These historical searches will reveal that some false details about our history are commonly held as the truth; while other historical data are accurate. We therefore must separate the false data from the true in order to fully realize how we got to the present time in such an economic mess. Be fully aware that when Continental Congress ratified the Constitution in 1787 nothing was done to correct a wrong path they had taken earlier. It was only a matter of time, not much at that, for avaricious men to buy off enough of our elected officials in order to take over this authority to create money and charge interest for its use. We got to this place because men like Benjamin Franklin and Alexander Hamilton promoted the usury system in money creation. This is not saying Jefferson didn't consent to their practice of usury. But at least Jefferson warned America about allowing the private bankers to have this power to issue our currency.

Where did they go wrong? There is a financial history book that has survived on a University of Michigan library shelf. Google has scanned the entire book and makes it available as free viewing at Google Books with the following url: http://books.google.com/books/about/Financial_History_of_the_ United_States.html?id=l3oaAAAAMAAJ . The first 57 pages cover the early history of all three periods. On pages 279 through 293 there is revealing information about the Civil War period that we will analyze a little further on herein. But history of the earliest period in Puritan New England shows that some public officials were dead set against allowing usury in their colony. John Cotton and Governor John Winthrop of Massachusetts were among those anti-usury Puritans. [14] [15] Now just about three generations later one Josiah (Benjamin) Franklin was born in 1706 when a new school of thought about usury was taking root among his generation of Puritans. Franklin turned out to be in favor of charging moderate interest rates on loans to the people by the government for the paper currency they issued. He published his essay favoring paper currency and usury in 1729. [16] During the 18th century Colonial governments discovered paper currency and emitted "Bills of Credit" as loans to the people at interest from which it was believed relief would come for government expenditures. Many today think all this Colonial Scrip that was issued was of the sort that was paid into existence for the expenditures of government. To an extent this was true in some cases. Usually about eight percent of the emission was used for this purpose. The rest was lent to colonial borrowers at interest. The Colonial governments took in the usury as a revenue source.

But notice also that as these loans were paid back, more money disappeared from the currency stream than was issued as loans. Additional money from around the world was circulating in the colonies from which the interest had to be captured. These were competing currencies that were in circulation ; one of them was piece of eight real. [17] Thus, many have bought into a belief that the colonies experienced prosperity during these times ; and that this prosperity was the result of issuing their own currency. But do read those first 57 pages of Dewey's book to get the straight facts about the Scrip. Things were rosy at times and not so rosy at other times. There were periods of inflation in which the Scrip became worth next to nothing. But Franklin was a great salesman and promoted his propaganda very successfully ; and so it became the venom that eventually shut down everyone else's moral compass. There was then, as now, very few who could grasp what a great bane upon civilization usury would morph into.

We now should easily be able to comprehend that an 1892 declaration from the US Supreme court was a bogus claim: The Supreme Court determined and declared the United States was indeed a Christian Nation. As jurists on that court, they had no excuse for neglecting numerous Christian Biblical interdictions prohibiting any usury, especially domestically. Howard B. Rand was indeed a jurist who was head and shoulders above almost every attorney ever to have lived in this nation. Perhaps Ellen Brown is almost ready to notice that if a government of, for and by the people can create the money that is a necessary component as a medium of exchange in a successful commercial system, then it can create money to both pay for governmental administrative expenditures and infrastructures ; and it can also lend it usury free to all. If our National Credit Agency took on the name **Public Bank** in Ellen's honor, so be it, as long as usury became prohibited on simple loan contracts and the Public Bank took on the responsibility of lending, asking for nothing in return.

Private banking would consequently be reduced to money handling services charging fees only. As accountants they have proved themselves capable of tracking the minutest details, and could be contracted to administer the NCA's usury free credit card division. They would, of course, be paid from direct credit emissions (in legal tender notes) so that no fees collected from the borrowers would even be necessary. It would be a great victory for the kingdom of heaven to have usury on simple loans, homestead mortgages, student and business loans eliminated across the entire nation. If there are bankers desirous of bringing in a return on money that they actually possess, then let them become involved in mutual risk contracts putting their own assets or real capital up as collateral.

As further validation that the Constitution gives Congress the authority to create money, we fast-forward here to 1861 when treasury secretary Salmon P. Chase used this power to issue about

$450 Million in demand notes as legal tender for the payment of public dues. We should observe here some excerpts from Davis Rich Dewey's book. He was an economics professor at MIT whose narrative in *Financial History of the United States* [18] gives a detailed account for this Civil War period. The important excerpts will be consolidated here. They may be rather lengthy ; but they give details which precisely validate that Constitutionally, Congress alone has this power to issue legal tender notes and credit - not a privately owned banking cartel.

Underlining is added herein only for the purpose of our study. The underlining is not part of Dewey's original text.

From pages 279 through 283:

"But it was agreed that the banks should be the medium of popular subscriptions through which the burden was to be transferred to private lenders. The inherent difficulty of carrying out the plan was great ; and it was increased by differences as to the <u>meaning of the agreement between the government and banks</u>. In order to prevent the removal of a large volume of <u>money</u> from the channels of business, the banks desired that the <u>funds,</u> which they loaned to the government, should remain <u>in their custody</u> until checked out by the government to meet current disbursements. This meant, of course, that the banks would be permitted to use their notes in the payment of treasury checks. <u>Under the sub-treasury act only coin was receivable by the treasury</u>, but the existing public distrust had caused <u>hoarding</u>, and there was a relatively small amount of <u>specie</u> (gold coin) then available in the country ; hence the transfer of so large a sum as $150 Million in gold was regarded

by many experts as impracticable. It was indeed asserted that the act of August 5, 1861 (amending the loan act of July 17), in allowing "the secretary of the treasury to deposit any of the moneys obtained on any of the loans now authorized by law, to the credit of the treasurer of the United States, in such solvent specie-paying banks as he may select," <u>was intended to give the secretary elastic powers to receive bank bills or book credit</u> (These are respectively bank paper currency and bank ledger credit in typical fractional reserve fashion. In **Part II** we will learn what Thomas Jefferson wrote about this bank paper currency – or as he put it bank notes. Dewey here refers to them as bank bills.) *in place of coin. James Gallatin, representing some New York banks, declared "that this provision was particularly intended to authorize drafts for disbursements against the deposits created by the taking of loans."* (This can be likened to modern commercial paper or a mortgage. In other words, it is the collateral used to secure bank credit.) *The secretary, however, strictly construed the sub-treasury bill and insisted that the banks should make their settlements in specie.*

<u>*"Another ground of remonstrance by bankers was Chase's free use of his power to issue demand notes; these notes were legal tender for payment of public dues; and if they went largely into circulation the banks*</u>

Continued on Page 30.

28

Bankers Oppression Chart
30-Year Mortgage

Principal Amount $	Interest Rate	No. of Payments	Monthly Payment Amount $	Months to Pay Back Initial Principal	Years to Pay Back Initial Principal	Total Paid After 20 Years $	Total Paid After 30 Years $
$100,000	3 ½ %	360	449.04	222.7	18.56	107,770	161,654
100,000	4 %	360	477.42	209.5	17.45	114,581	171,871
100,000	4 ½ %	360	506.69	197.4	16.45	121606	182,408
100,000	5 %	360	536.83	186.3	15.52	128,839	193,259
100,000	5 ½ %	360	567.79	176.1	14.68	136,270	204,404
100,000	6 %	360	599.56	166.8	13.9	145,682	215,842
100,000	6 ½ %	360	632.07	158.2	13.18	153,413	227,545
100,000	7 %	360	665.31	150.3	12.53	161,314	239,512
100,000	7 ½ %	360	699.22	143	11.92	167,813	251,719
100,000	8 %	360	733.77	136.3	11.36	176,105	264,157
100,000	8 ½ %	360	768.92	130.05	10.84	184,541	276,811
100,000	9 %	360	804.63	124.28	10.36	193,111	289,667
100,000	9 ½ %	360	840.86	118.93	9.91	201,806	302,710
100,000	10 %	360	877.58	113.95	9.5	210,619	315,929

For all who are not familiar with how banks create new money with a bank credit double entry system of accounting, we need to firmly fix in our minds that banks do not really have money of their own to lend out at interest. So we assert here and now that banks put up very little in any loan contract because borrowers put up their assets as the collateral of the loan that brings the new money into existence. Sure, the banks have a building, some employees and some business equipment to do the accounting. All businesses have these costs. But it is patently obvious that when compared with any manufacturing facility, they have very little at risk. They need neither raw materials, nor automation machinery, nor a delivery system to bring their product to market.

A debenture brings this money into existence out of nothing. Moreover, it is exactly the same set of conditions that a gold owner uses to bring new money into being. The claim is made that gold backs their credit creations. But where is their gold kept during the term of any loan contract? Is their gold ever at risk during any loan contract? The answer to this question is unequivocally no. As usual, it is the borrower who stands to lose not only the property involved in the loan transaction, but also all the payments made over the course of the loan and all the up front fees that were required of the borrower in order that the loan would be processed. These are questions never asked nor ever answered by the folks at DailyBell.com or LewRockwell.com . Furthermore, these home mortgages are really just small potatoes when compared with what is going on with commercial papers in manufacturing.

When a mortgage contract or a commercial paper is signed by both a lender and a borrower, brand new money comes into existence and enters the currency stream. This new money (the principle of the loan) cancels out of existence as it is paid back. When it cancels out, it is eliminated from the money supply. We should observe that as loans are paid off, a contraction of the money supply occurs because, in addition to the principle, interest must also be paid. Thus banks have the capability to either expand or contract the money supply to suit their own selfish purposes by issuing or not issuing new credit to compensate for the interest due from previous loans. These antics and acts of legerdemain they perform are accomplished very discretely and in ways so that very few are wise enough to detect it.

Notice also that a six percent interest rate on loans is one that Ben Franklin considered reasonable. By today's standards, someone with an original principal amount of $100,000 actually borrowed around $95,000 to $97,000. They normally would need to pay $3,000 to $5,000 in mortgage discount points to secure the loan depending on whether or not the borrower put up a down payment. Additionally, there are up front fees the borrower always pays for and the initial principal amount may even be higher, thus causing the payments to be somewhat higher than what a borrower anticipated.

During the 1980s, after the Carter administration left us with his legacy of near hyperinflation, mortgage interest rates of 10 % and even higher were common. We mention this because there are those naïve social credit economists who think that a dividend directly to the people will not somehow be simply nullified by bankers who will raise interest rates. You see, the social crediters are intent on leaving the charging of usury on loans as is.

Now we should also observe that just because gold owners have many people hoodwinked into believing the money they create is not fiat money, doesn't mean that it isn't. They are indeed wizards who continue to try and baffle as many simple minded as they can with their trick discussions. The real truth is that they create new money upon which interest must be paid on top of the principal. How does that differ from money say that our government would create based upon the full faith and credit of the people whose assets and labor would be the backing?

Thomas Edison noted in the 1920s that the Constitution that makes the Treasury Bonds good would also make Treasury Notes good. Only in the case of the Notes, there is no usury to be paid to bankers. Notes would have paid for the Mussel Shoals dam project as direct credit emissions without having a middleman who owns a bank create our notes for us at interest. If our Constitution provides the people with the authority to create our money as direct credit emissions, then why don't the elected hypocrites in government comply?

A National Credit Authority instituted for the principles of purpose enumerated in the Unanimous Declaration and Preamble to fund all levels of government – military, police, emergency management, pensions, welfare as well as a bureaucracy commissioned to administer interest free loans for domestic businesses, student loans and primary residence home mortgages – is all that is necessary to establish an adequate money supply. And to keep the money supply in balance with the GDP, a flat rate increase tax is the only tax needed. All other taxation is only a scapegoat to fleece the people.

The Austrian schoolers want to gain sole control of our nation's monetary system. They call themselves libertarians. What they want is liberty for themselves to keep everyone else in debt slavery – economic bondage.

30

Continued From Page 27.

would naturally receive less gold in their daily business transactions, and *thus would be less able to fulfill their loan agreement with the government.* *Some bankers asserted that the secretary had promised not to use this power.* *At first the notes were issued in moderation, but in November the secretary gave way to what he considered the imperative claims of the treasury and put out notes freely, on the ground that Congress had ordered appropriations beyond those estimated in the summer, and that the revenues from imports did not come up to the estimates ; he saw no other relief. In spite of the differences of opinion, banks for a time continued to co-operate with the treasury department in carrying out the original agreement for the purchase of bonds.*

"In connection with a request for authority to make further loans of $200 million the secretary advanced his first proposals for a national banking system. He believed that the time had come when Congress should exercise its authority over the credit circulation of the country. He thought his plan would give the following advantages : (1) uniformity of circulation, in place of a bank-note circulation dependent on the laws of 34 States and 1600 private corporations (Which bank notes in reality manifest as the anarchy that follows such a broad array of independent actions.) *; (2) an increased security to the Union, because of a common interest created by the disposition of national securities as a basis of*

circulation ; (3) the safest currency the country had ever enjoyed. Little emphasis was laid on the special demand for <u>United States stock</u> as a basis of bank circulation, but this advantage evidently was a strong reason for making the recommendation. Chase did not refer to the recent controversy with the banks, nor did he specially discuss the issue of the demand notes ; on the general question of government paper currency he did call attention to the inconveniences and hazards of the issue of United States notes, possibly ending in the '<u>immeasurable evils</u> of dishonest public faith and national bankruptcy'.

121. Suspension of Specie Payments

"Although the secretary did not officially take notice of the growing embarrassments of the banks, bankers found them very serious ; and on December 30 (1861), under the lead of the New York City banks, specie (gold) payments were suspended throughout the country ; and this action was speedily followed by the government. This sudden and eventful shock to private and public credit has been the subject of much controversy. Chase declared that suspension was inevitable, because of unexpected military reverses, increased expenditures, and diminished confidence in public securities ; and in this conclusion Republican leaders of the time acquiesced ; they denied that the issue of <u>demand notes</u> in any way caused suspension, since only $33.46 million was in circulation at the date of suspension, and up to

that day every note presented for payment had been promptly redeemed in coin.

"On the other hand the bankers declared that the two reasons for the suspension were first, the pressure on banks because they were not allowed to retain the government deposits received in the loan operations until they were actually needed ; and second, the banks were expected by their customers to receive the <u>government demand notes</u> *for deposit, and permit them to be drawn against in coin ; and such a burden the banks affirmed was too heavy to carry. They therefore laid upon Chase the responsibility for the suspension of specie payments :*

"The <u>demand notes</u> not only irritated the banks, they also held an important relation in subsequent discussion to the <u>legal tenders</u> and the agitation for <u>fiat money</u>. After the suspension of specie payments these notes which were receivable <u>for all public dues</u>, circulated at a premium over <u>State bank-notes</u> and also over the <u>treasury notes</u> or <u>greenbacks</u>, which were issued the following year but were not made receivable for customs."

This ends a long quote from Dr. Dewey's book. One sentence needs to be restated here so that we can grasp that even some of what a Ph. D. offered us as analysis may not have even been fully understood by himself:

"In order to prevent the removal of a large volume of <u>money</u> from the channels of business, the banks desired that the <u>funds,</u> which they loaned to the government,

should remain in their custody until checked out by the government to meet current disbursements."

We ask here and now "what funds"? Were these funds the imaginary funds bankers create as **bank credit** in their signed agreements? As such, he classifies the funds as money. We can easily glean from reading carefully near the beginning of the Dewey quote that bank credit was a private bank feature in common use during this epoch. Dewey called it 'book credit'. Earlier herein we learned that **bank credit** very much operates in the same way as fiat money or paper currency. The nation's money supply expands and contracts as **bank credit** is either freely given or curtailed. The Bank of England, a privately owned bank, had been doing something similar with wooden tallies since 1694. The American Colonies had been doing this same thing with 'bills of credit' as paper currency.

So we must ask ourselves thus: what exactly from these excerpts of Dewey's book is easily understandable about greenbacks? There is much to comprehend even without analysis of all the paper currency's features. That some of the greenback issues were convertible into bonds is of minor consequence. That wage inflation did not keep up with the incipient price inflation is also of minor consequence. This, in fact, was likely caused by competing bank credit and bank notes issued from the private sector anyway. Perhaps Chase was very close to being correct about a national bank and should have sought for legislation to revoke the ability of banks to issue their own credit and notes. More significant aspects of the greenbacks issue by treasury are twofold: first, Dewey admits about the Constitutional authority of Congress to issue the demand notes as legal tender to pay for public dues, and second, Dewey noted in more than one place that the bankers were against the government using this power because, even then, they were intent on reserving this power for themselves alone. The culmination of their intrigue became manifest when willing dupes among our elected beltway officials inaugurated the privately owned Federal Reserve. **(18)** In reading all of Dewey's narrative on this critical period of American history, we will find that these greenbacks did circulate among the population for a time as money, proving that all the people really need for commerce is an adequate medium of exchange, not a fungible based upon usury that is released into circulation by the systematized, institutional anarchy bankers seek to perpetuate. This truly is an accurate description of what **bank credit** accomplishes: economic anarchy.

The Christian Bible on Money
Vs. the Constitution

There are a few Bible believing Christians who are aware that there are some defects in our Constitution. Most notable are a slew of egregious, unneeded Amendments along with the clause in Article 1 Section 8 Line 1 allowing Congress to borrow. This clause must be nullified with an Amendment. If Congress has the authority to create money, why should it borrow any? In fact, in Line 5 of the same section, the word "coin" should be amended to read "create" or "coin and create". There really is no need to scrap the Unanimous Declaration of Independence, the Preamble and the Bill of Rights. Many people today fight tooth and nail against the plain intent embodied within the august pages of these documents. These three sets of documents stand firmly against oppression of the people by tyrants as a testament from numerous historical settings. They are the result of episodes from human experiences in which the majority of people were victims of despotism. Would we scrap such wisdom from epochs past in which valuable lessons are to be learned? We now experience this tyranny we have tried to avoid because we have neglected one last necessity for good government: only an honest monetary system will end the banking anarchy.

St. Paul wrote in 1 Timothy 6:10, *"For the love of money is the root of all evil: which while some coveted after, they have erred from the faith, and pierced themselves through with many sorrows."* If this Scripture gives an indication of what we open ourselves up to by elevating the status of money to become a fungible good, it should be evident as to exactly how thoroughly corrupt adversaries have been able to wrest complete control of the beltway elected buffoons. As long as honest citizens continue to beat around the bushes instead of directly confronting the root of their power, we will remain toothless tigers blowing smoke into the wind rather than kindling the fire that Jesus lit.

Thomas Jefferson provided us with keen enough insight showing us the first step that will be a necessary component of the total solution. His warning was, *"I believe that banking institutions are more dangerous to our liberties than standing armies. If the American people ever allow private banks to control the issue of their currency, first by inflation, then by deflation, the banks and corporations that will grow up around the banks will deprive the people of all property - until their children wake-up homeless on the continent their fathers conquered. The issuing power should be taken from the banks and restored to the people, to whom it properly belongs."* [19] The second step will be incorporating almighty God's interdiction against all usury on simple loans. It is also the reason that the moneychangers have been successful at wresting the political process out of our control. Working people now do not have the capability of funding a political campaign without kow towing to the moneychangers. We thus have lost all three branches of our government to the moneyed elite. What did we expect when we decided to ignore the most important of almighty God's laws on commerce and finance, the law against usury?

Almost everything contained within the context of our founding documents can be validated within the pages of the Bible. But the founders erred greatly on usury. Jesus Himself, a long time ago, approved of all righteousness, even the righteousness of non-Christians in Matthew 10:41, *"He who receives a prophet in the name of a prophet shall receive a prophet's reward. And he who receives a **righteous man** in the name of a **righteous man** shall receive a **righteous man**'s reward."* We are thus encouraged to select people for elected service as judges based on their commitment to almighty God's eternal moral laws, rather than their education or a religion they may wear on their sleeve. We need a **Jury System** in which once per year new **Jurists** are selected from among the population to audit government activity, and to judge the law itself, and to weed out malfeasance. This **Jury** will be charged with upholding the highest ideals embodied within the pages of the Christian Bible. The basis for this **Jury** branch of government with the ability as final arbiter over any of the other three branches is rooted also in the Bible from the 400 year period of Judges, and whereby Jesus Christ will be the head of our government as King.

Social Credit

Let us now also consider Major Clifford Hugh Douglas, a Scottish engineer who proposed a monetary innovation during the 1920s. It was his opinion that a dividend should be given to citizens free and clear as compensation for the shortage of money that always exists in people's purchasing power. This shortage really does exist by reason of the way money is created as credit that must be repaid with interest. Whenever a loan is retired the principal disappears from existence. But the interest that is paid to retire the loan is only allowed into the currency stream as the result of another loan. So to pay off one loan, additional loans must always be issued or there would not be enough money to pay interest. This is easily shown in an exponential graph in which debt always increases as principal plus interest is paid back. Debt cannot ever be paid off and it is ever increasing. So Douglas discovered this and devised his own innovation to compensate for it. For some reason, he decided not to battle against the money power and how usury on simple loans is the real problem. Rather, he sought to promote his own system that amounts to being nothing more than a palliative approach. Meanwhile, the ancient books of the Bible have shown the correct solution for many centuries. Furthermore, many other passages in the Bible definitely show that a Douglas dividend would be very unwise. Endnote [20] shows Scriptural citations that speak for themselves in opposition to CH Douglas's approach. Endless, fruitless discussions with those whose wisdom is not influenced by Jesus or God's moral law can be a waste of efforts. But very simply, slothfulness, drunkenness and criminal inclination have never been identified as virtues.

What can we observe here? There are, no doubt, people in the Social Credit Google forum who honestly believe the Christian faith supports their objective that a dividend should be given to everyone, even criminals, drug addicts, alcoholics and shiftless sluggards, none of whom can keep a job, many of whom do not even want a job. Mankind has not yet even gotten a handle on evil in the world. Should we be suckers and reward evildoers? We need to make God's righteous moral laws our priority, first and foremost, not make sure that everyone gets their share of free money. What exactly is wrong in requiring individuals to do something useful in exchange for their earnings?

Douglas also suggested another perk to individual citizens in his monetary proposals. He called it a compensated price (CP) mechanism utilizing his credit system to make sure that just prices are charged when consumers make retail purchases. There is nothing wrong in ensuring that consumers aren't ripped off. Douglas's CP is an attempt to codify and regulate unscrupulous manufacturers and retailers by giving additional free credit to consumers. Here again we find another palliative approach as a solution rather than prohibiting price scalping. In fact, Hoffman showed that early Puritan and Thomistic economics were not negligent in addressing this issue. [21] So this particular societal problem was attended to long before Douglas noticed the inherent lack of purchasing power among the general population.

One problem with CH Douglas is that he possibly thought his monetary system would somehow mitigate the effects of usury as long as everyone gets free money. Instead of doing a full-bore charge against the amoral practice of charging interest on simple loan contracts, he got a brainstorm idea of institutionalizing a National Credit Dividend as well as CP. But if this system of his is contrary to that which the Christian Bible has taught for many centuries, how can they declare that Douglas economics satisfies Christian ethics? They seem to think that Douglas's philosophy will magically cause evil to disappear or at least become less costly. Evil is always a logical choice for many ; their brains just work that way ; and they must be dealt with collectively through what? A government? How do we fund that government? What will occur, though, is that the sluggards, users and alcoholics will be paid at least twice for their wayward ways: once with the dividend and then again when they are old and infirm and haven't provided themselves with any pension or savings. So then the people will pay for their food, shelter and medical care the second time around all over again.

Those who embrace the teachings of CH Douglas with all their hearts have no doubt missed or ignored the twenty seven Bible passages shown in endnote [20] . Ignoring the wisdom written therein while we live in the age of human government can only lead us into one failed innovation after another.

Furthermore, a failure to prohibit usury will nullify any positive effects Social Credit may directly give simply because those who set interest rates will just raise the rates. And beyond the obvious enabling advantage usury gives to the money creators, people whose lives can be described as shipwreck will sink into a deeper dark hole when they are enabled by being given free money while reciprocating nothing useful in return for it.

Proverbs 14:12
There is a way which seemeth right unto a man, but the end thereof are the ways of death.
Proverbs 16:25
There is a way which seemeth right unto a man, but the end thereof are the ways of death.

Conclusion

Usury on simple loan contracts has always been the cause of economic oppression. And it still is. Usury makes a **fungible** out of money. Without usury, money would merely be a medium of exchange. What is really needed to eliminate barter? When we choose to use money as a fungible, we do it this way to satisfy our baser instincts like avarice, greed and lust. But without the usury in moneylending we open up an entirely new world of opportunity for everyone. Retail prices on goods and services would be more in alignment with what working people can afford. All taxes but a tax on increase would be done away with. The pages of the Bible thus show us a world of hope ahead, if we would only choose to look seriously at the very simple economic model God gave to Moses three and a half millennia ago. Please read carefully Leviticus chapter 25 **[10]**. As long ago as that was written, economic oppression was emphatically the reason the law against usury was committed to writing. That is why there should also be forgiveness on loans for disaster victims and unfortunate catastrophic illness. All these clauses were codified in the Mosaic

Law. No doubt, even way back then, the overlooking Divine providence was a guiding light in the formation of Ancient Israel's constitution. Should we ignore, as did the ancient Israelites, these ways that were mapped out for them while we ourselves deliberate with our own initiatives to bring about good government?

Gertrude Coogan's solutions in ***Money Creators*** somewhat mirror what's included in the model I described above ; except she made no mention of usury free lending. In fact Coogan, like Jefferson, approved of usury lending, as long as the lender has real capital to lend. This simply means 'book' or 'bank' credit would be prohibited in her system. So Coogan's model would satisfy a good measure of the three needed elements; but she missed the target Biblically on usury.

Liam Allone's model (www.economicdemocracy.com) presented in ***Economic Cures "They" Don't Want You to Know About*** also identifies much of what is lacking in Douglas's vision. But he suggests usury free lending to only corporations in his model. Even this would be a step forward. But he, too, falls short of establishing an honest monetary system by allowing bankers to continue in their 'book' credit at interest scam.

Doctors and dentists purchase equipment for their practices, as do contractors and mechanics. All the principal plus interest they pay for their equipment, for the homes they live in and for the education of their offspring must be captured from the prices they charge to their customers. If they all could obtain front capital usury free for whatever their purposes are, would the retail prices they charge reflect the lowered costs? Usury free lending to all is the major element of what is needed not only to bring success, it would also end economic oppression of the whole population. And we would also be acknowledging that two thousand years ago one person with the name of Jesus Christ has been right all along.

Therefore, until the time arrives in which the charging of

interest on all simple loans is prohibited, and in which the authority to create our money is taken away from corporate anarchists who run the private banks, and thus restored back to Congress with the outlawing of usury, this nation cannot be styled as something it never was: Christian.

Endnotes

[1]
< **http://en.wikipedia.org/wiki/Coin** >

[2]
< **http://en.wikipedia.org/wiki/Medium_of_exchange** >
Hopefully the reader will eventually begin to see what is missing in these Wikipedia entries. They make a simple subject not easily understandable for some. But eventually, when our ability to interpret economics data becomes proficient, we will begin to easily understand everything they deliberately do not explain.
 http://en.wikipedia.org/wiki/Greenback_(money)
The term greenback refers to paper currency (printed in green on one side) issued by the United States during the American Civil War. They were in two forms: Demand Notes, issued in 1861-1862, and United States Notes issued in 1862-1865. They were legal tender by law, but were not backed by gold or silver.

[3]
< https://archive.org/details/MoneyCreators > PDF - Pages 46 and 47. If the reader has available the book version the same is found on page 84. *Hidden Mysteries – TGS Publishers*, 22241 Pinedale Lane, Frankston, Texas 75763. *Money Creators* 2006.
(903) 876 3256
www.hiddenmysteries.com
info@hiddenmysteries.com

[4]
< http://en.wikipedia.org/wiki/Fiat_money >

[5]
< http://en.wikipedia.org/wiki/Contract_Clause >

[6]   1. < http://en.wikipedia.org/wiki/Bills_of_credit >

2. *Financial History of the United States* PDF Pages 1 through 57. by Davis Rich Dewey, PH.D., LL.D. – 1915, Professor of Economics and Statistics – Massachusetts Institute of Technology.

[7]
< http://en.wikipedia.org/wiki/Greenback_(money) >
< http://en.wikipedia.org/wiki/Bills_of_credit >

Two links are shown here in which contradictory information is given in Wikipedia.   An historian who wrote the data in the Greenbacks Wikipedia link noted that these were the only paper currency issued by the United States. (This was during the Civil War only.) But earlier on in history in the American Colonies, Continental Congress and even post-1787 with the First Bank of the United States, 'Bills of Credit' were also issued as money. In fact even Wikipedia's article on the Bills of Credit calls them money. The discrepancy is resolved in Dewey's *Financial History of the United States*, pages 1 through 57.

[8]

Edison Explains Money

(Transcribed from The Spotlight, Liberty Lobby from an August 1983 Issue. The Spotlight is now known as American Free Press)
This is what America's populist inventor, Thomas Edison, had to say about our impossible monetary system. He made the remarks while discussing the proposed Mussel Shoals Dam electric power project.

By Thomas A. Edison

People who will not turn a shovel full of dirt on the project, nor contribute a pound of material, will collect more money from the United States than will the people who supply all the material and do all the work. This is the terrible thing about interest... But here is the point: If the nation can issue a dollar bond it can issue a dollar bill. The element that makes the bond good makes the bill good also. The difference between the bond and the bill is that the bond lets the money broker collect twice the amount of the bond and an additional 20 percent. Whereas the currency – the honest sort provided by the Constitution – pays nobody but those who contribute in some useful way. It is absurd to say our country can issue bonds and cannot issue currency. Both are promises to pay, but one fattens the usurer and the other helps the people. If the currency issued by the people were not good, then the bonds would be not good either. It is a terrible situation when the government, to insure the national wealth, must go in debt and submit to ruinous interest charges at the hands of men who control the fictitious value of gold. Interest is the invention of Satan.

[9]
< http://en.wikipedia.org/wiki/Bank_credit >

[10]
Leviticus 25:35-39 NKJV *35* " 'If one of your brethren becomes poor, and falls into poverty among you, then you shall help him,

like a stranger or a sojourner, that he may live with you. **36** Take no usury or interest from him; but fear your God, that your brother may live with you. **37** You shall not lend him your money for usury, nor lend him your food at a profit. **38** I am the Lord your God, who brought you out of the land of Egypt, to give you the land of Canaan and to be your God. **39** 'And if one of your brethren who dwells by you becomes poor, and sells himself to you, you shall not compel him to serve as a slave."

Deuteronomy 15:1-11 NKJV "At the end of every seven years you shall grant a release of debts. **2** And this is the form of the release: Every creditor who has lent anything to his neighbor shall release it; he shall not require it of his neighbor or his brother, because it is called the Lord's release. **3** Of a foreigner you may require it; but you shall give up your claim to what is owed by your brother, **4** except when there may be no poor among you; for the Lord will greatly bless you in the land which the Lord your God is giving you to possess as an inheritance— **5** only if you carefully obey the voice of the Lord your God, to observe with care all these commandments which I command you today. **6** For the Lord your God will bless you just as He promised you; you shall lend to many nations, but you shall not borrow; you shall reign over many nations, but they shall not reign over you. **7** "If there is among you a poor man of your brethren, within any of the gates in your land which the Lord your God is giving you, you shall not harden your heart nor shut your hand from your poor brother, **8** but you shall open your hand wide to him and willingly lend him sufficient for his need, whatever he needs. **9** Beware lest there be a wicked thought in your heart, saying, 'The seventh year, the year of release, is at hand,' and your eye be evil against your poor brother and you give him nothing, and he cry out to the Lord against you, and it become sin among you. **10** You shall surely give to him, and your heart should not be grieved when you give to him, because for this thing the Lord your God will bless you in all your works and in all to which you put your hand.

11 For the poor will never cease from the land; therefore I command you, saying, 'You shall open your hand wide to your brother, to your poor and your needy, in your land.'"

Deuteronomy 23:19,20 NKJV "**19** "You shall not charge interest to your brother—interest on money or food or anything that is lent out at interest. **20** To a foreigner you may charge interest, but to your brother you shall not charge interest, that the Lord your God may bless you in all to which you set your hand in the land which you are entering to possess."

This is the place in all Bible translations where readers are cautioned not to misinterpret the passage without first learning the difference between 'ger' and 'nokri'. There were foreigners living peaceably within the borders of greater ancient Israel that were comparable with a modern term we use known as 'resident aliens'. These resident aliens who lived there, who loved the Lord and God's people were to be treated as any of the Israelites with respect to this law against usury.

PSALM 15:1-5 NKJV Lord, who may abide in Your tabernacle? Who may dwell in Your holy hill?

2 He who walks uprightly,   And works righteousness,   And speaks the truth in his heart;

3 He who does not backbite with his tongue,   Nor does evil to his neighbor,   Nor does he take up a reproach against his friend;

4 In whose eyes a vile person is despised,   But he honors those who fear the Lord; He who swears to his own hurt and does not change;

5 He who does not put out his money at usury,   Nor does he take a bribe against the innocent.

He who does these things shall never be moved.

Ezechiel 22:12 NKJV 12 In you they take bribes to shed blood; you take usury and increase; you have made profit from your neighbors by extortion, and have forgotten Me," says the Lord God."

Luke 6:35 NKJV "But love your enemies, do good, and lend, hoping for nothing in return; and your reward will be great, and you will be sons of the Most High. For He is kind to the unthankful and evil."

46

We can also add here that on pages 202 and 203 of *Usury in Christendom* Michael Hoffman adds numerous additional references of synods and councils in which the practice of usury in moneylending was strictly condemned by and earlier faithful Apostolic Christian church. Here are a few: The first Nicene Council canon 17; first Carthage Council cap. 13; first Lateran Council; Council of Vienne; Eliberine Council, St Augustine, St. Bernard and Thomas Aquinas.

[11]
We Christians today must begin (or at least those of us who pay attention) at the point from which Jesus addressed Pharisees and lawyers as those who teach doctrines of men instead of using the plain intent written in Scripture. And, if Jesus truly is God incarnate, then every word He spoke carries the weight of our responsibility. We either choose to follow Him, or we choose what the educators and gainsayers (the modern Pharisees and lawyers) have said that it is okay for us to do.

Proverbs 30:5 "Every word of God is pure: he is a shield unto them that put their trust in him."

Mark 7:11-13 "But ye say, If a man shall say to his father or mother, It is Corban, that is to say, a gift, by whatsoever thou mightest be profited by me; he shall be free. And ye suffer him no more to do ought for his father or his mother; Making the word of God of none effect through your tradition, which ye have delivered: and many such like things do ye."

Luke 3:2 "while Annas and Caiaphas were high priests, the word of God came to John the son of Zacharias in the wilderness."

Luke 4:4 "And Jesus answered him, saying, It is written, That man shall not live by bread alone, but by every word of God."

Luke 5:1 "And it came to pass, that, as the people pressed upon him to hear the word of God, he stood by the lake of Gennesaret,"

Luke 8:11 "Now the parable is this: The seed is the word of God."

Luke 8:21 "And he answered and said unto them, My mother and my brethren are these which hear the word of God, and do it."

Luke 11:28 "But he said, Yea rather, blessed are they that hear the word of God, and keep it. John 10:35 If he called them gods, unto whom the word of God came, and the scripture cannot be broken;"

Acts 4:31 "And when they had prayed, the place was shaken where they were assembled together; and they were all filled with the Holy Ghost, and they spake the word of God with boldness."

[12]
Here is an excerpt from pages 118, 119 of Gertrude Coogan's book *Money Creators*:

"Banking, as it is conducted in the United States today (1935) is actually a conspiracy operating against society. It is operated to periodically destroy property values, and disastrously curtail income, wages and profits; under control of the 'Federal' Banks, loading upon the people the maximum possible burden of tribute in the way of interest, both public and private. The maxim is, 'Make the nation carry the maximum amount of interest possible. Keep the masses paying interest to the privileged few.' Interest is simply the overwhelming tribute which all of the producers of real wealth in the nation are paying to a few who enjoy the unconstitutional and dishonest privilege of creating money.

"Note carefully that the original issuance or creation of money, paid into circulation, should always be interest free. Carefully distinguish this original issuance of money upon its creation with the lending of real money, which has been obtained by those who have earned it by rendering personal services or real goods in exchange for that money."

[13]
What follows here is a newspaper blog by US Senator Carl Levin from September 2013. And here is the senator's opening sentence, "In August, I led a bipartisan group of Senate colleagues in introducing a bill to combat terrorism, money laundering, tax evasion, and other wrongdoing aided by use of U.S. corporations with hidden owners." We must remember that political tripe like this, that the senator releases, is only for public consumption. Judging from shareholder ownership in important corporations like military/defense contractors and public utilities as being majority held by banking and fund institutions, he did not note that these also would be dealt with in his proposed legislation. Nowhere in it did he mention that the Wall Street bankers would also be prohibited from anonymously owning shell corporations that they have been lending to for at least a century with money they can create out of nothing. In all, probably this will be the last we hear about this proposed legislation. When the Wall Street lawyers learn that one of their own shills is attempting to put a stop to anonymously owning shell corporations, an escape clause will most likely be snuck into the draft of the legislation.

Bill Would End Corporate Secrecy
to Fight Terrorism, Crime
By Carl Levin
September 2013

"In August I led a bipartisan group of Senate colleagues in introducing a bill to combat terrorism, money laundering, tax evasion, and other wrongdoing aided by use of corporations with hidden owners. This common sense bill would stop our states from forming about two million new corporations each year for unidentified owners, and instead require those applying to form a new corporation to list the owners behind it so that, if misconduct later occurred, law enforcement could track down the wrongdoers.

"The bill, which I introduced with sens. Chuck Grassley, Dianne Feinstein and Tom Harkin, has the support of the Federal Law Enforcement officers Association, the Fraternal Order of Police, the National Association of Assistant United States Attorneys, and the Society of Former Special Agents of the Federal Bureau of Investigation.

"Law enforcement groups support our bill because right now in the United States it takes more information to get a driver's license or to open a bank account than to form a corporation. Our bill would change that by requiring any state that accepts crime-fighting grants from the Department of Justice to add one new question to their existing incorporation forms, asking applicants to identify the company's true owners.

"That's it. One simple question. But it's an important one.

"Why? To begin with, we know some terrorists and criminals use U.S. corporations to carry out their activities. Viktor Bout, an arms dealer who was found guilty in November 2011 of conspiring to kill U.S. nationals and selling weapons to a terrorist organization, used corporations around the world in his work, including a dozen formed in Texas, Delaware and Florida. It is unacceptable that Bout was able to set up corporations in three states and use them in illicit activities without ever being asked for his name. In another case, a New York company called Assa Corp. owned a Manhattan skyscraper and in 2007 transferred about $4.5 million in rental payments to a bank in Iran. U.S. law enforcement officers tracking the funds had no idea who was behind that corporation until another government disclosed that it was owned by the Alavi Foundation, which had ties to the Iranian military. In other words, a New York corporation was being used to ship millions of dollars to Iran, a notorious supporter of terrorism.

"U.S. corporations with hidden owners have also been involved in financial crimes. In 2011, a former Russian military officer, Victor Kaganov, pleaded guilty to operating an illegal money-transfer business from his home in Oregon and using Oregon shell corporations to wire more that $150 million around the world on behalf of Russian clients.

"Shell corporations are also notorious for their role in health care fraud. One example involves an individual named Michel Huarte who formed 29 shell companies in several states including Florida, Louisiana and North Carolina and used them to make fraudulent health care claims, bilking Medicare out of more than $50 million.

"In these and other cases, great law enforcement work eventually pierced the veil of corporate secrecy. But that's not always what happens. In October 2004, the Homeland Security Department's division of Immigration and Customs Enforcement identified a Utah corporation that had engaged in $150 million in suspicious transactions. ICE found that the corporation had been formed in Utah and was owned by two Panamanian holding corporations, all located at the same Panama City office.

"By 2005, ICE had located 800 U.S. corporations in nearly every state associated with the same shadowy group in Panama, but was unable to obtain the name of a single person who owned any one of the corporations. ICE had learned that the 800 corporations were associated with multiple U.S. investigations into tax fraud and other wrondoing, but no one had been able to find the corporate owners. The trail went cold, and ICE closed the case.

Our bill would not only help law enforcment in such cases, it would bring the United States into compliance with international standards requiring countries to obtain beneficial ownership information for the corporations they form.

"It would also make U.S. domestic practices consistent with U.S. foreign policy. The fact that we have corporate secrecy right here in our backyard contradicts U.S. efforts to end corporate secrecy offshore. All over the world, people are standing up and speaking out against shell corporations with hidden owners being used to commit wrongdoing. It is time Congress acted to ensure transparency in the formation of U.S. corporations."

"Carl Levin is the senior U.S. senator from Michigan.

"Read more columns from syndicated national writers as well as authors from our own communities at themacombdaily.com "

[14]
Usury in Christendom: The Mortal Sin That Was and Now is Not by Michael Hoffman, 2013. Pages 222, 226, 231, 236-241, 245, 252 and 259.

[15]
Heavenly Merchandize: How Religion Shaped Commerce in Puritan America by Mark Valeri, Princeton University Press, 2010. Page 67.

[16]
< http://etext.lib.virginia.edu/users/brock/webdoc6.html > - This one is Benjamin Franklin's *A Modest Enquiry into the Nature and Necessity of a Paper-Currency*. This web page is not in PDF. It must be copied and pasted from the web page to some text editor capable of rich text format. BFWW.

[17]
http://books.google.com/books/about/Financial_Histor y_of_the_United_States.html?id=l3oaAAAAMAAJ PDF - This *Financial History of the United States* was published in 1915 by a PH.D. MIT professor named Davis Rich Dewey. This is a Google Books free download. Doing a Google search for this title will disclose that there are actually more than one free downloads in PDF for this book.
Page 20.

[18]
Ibid. Pages 279-292.

[19]
http://foundersquotes.com/quotes/i-believe-that-banking-institutions-are-more-dangerous-to-our-liberties-than-standing-armies/#more-499
Year: 1802 **Context:** Letter to the Secretary of the Treasury Albert Gallatin

[20]
2 Thessalonians 3:10-13
"For even when we were with you, this we commanded you, that if any would not work, neither should he eat. For we hear that there are some which walk among you disorderly, working not at all, but are busybodies.

Now them that are such we command and exhort by our Lord Jesus Christ, that with quietness they work, and eat their own bread.

But ye, brethren, be not weary in well doing."

1 Timothy 5:8, 18
"But if any provide not for his own, and specially for those of his own house, he hath denied the faith, and is worse than an infidel.

For the scripture saith, Thou shalt not muzzle the ox that treadeth out the corn. And, The labourer is worthy of his reward."

2 Timothy 2:6 "The husbandman that laboureth must be first partaker of the fruits."

2 Timothy 3:13-17 "But evil men and seducers shall wax worse and worse, deceiving, and being deceived. But continue thou in the things which thou hast learned and hast been assured of, knowing of whom thou hast learned them; And that from a child thou hast known the holy scriptures, which are able to make thee wise unto salvation through faith which is in Christ Jesus. All scripture is given by inspiration of God, and is profitable for doctrine, for reproof, for correction, for instruction in righteousness: That the man of God may be perfect, thoroughly furnished unto all good works."

Hebrews 2:7 "Thou madest him a little lower than the angels; thou crownedst him with glory and honour, and didst set him over the works of thy hands."

Hebrews 6:12 "That ye be not slothful, but followers of them who through faith and patience inherit the promises."

Romans 12:11 "Not slothful in business; fervent in spirit; serving the Lord;"

Matthew 25:26 "His lord answered and said unto him, Thou wicked and slothful servant, thou knewest that I reap where I sowed not, and gather where I have not strawed:"

Ecclesiastes 10:18 "By much slothfulness the building decayeth; and through idleness of the hands the house droppeth through."

Proverbs 21:25 "The desire of the slothful killeth him; for his hands refuse to labour."

Proverbs 6:6 "Go to the ant, thou sluggard; consider her ways, and be wise:"

Proverbs 6:9 "How long wilt thou sleep, O sluggard? when wilt thou arise out of thy sleep?"

Proverbs 10:26 "As vinegar to the teeth, and as smoke to the eyes, so is the sluggard to them that send him."

Proverbs 13:4 "The soul of the sluggard desireth, and hath nothing: but the soul of the diligent shall be made fat."

Proverbs 20:4 "The sluggard will not plow by reason of the cold; therefore shall he beg in harvest, and have nothing."

Proverbs 26:16 "The sluggard is wiser in his own conceit than seven men that can render a reason."

Proverbs 12:24 "The hand of the diligent shall bear rule: but the slothful shall be under tribute."

Proverbs 12:27 "The slothful man roasteth not that which he took in hunting: but the substance of a diligent man is precious."

Proverbs 15:19 "The way of the slothful man is as an hedge of thorns: but the way of the righteous is made plain."

Proverbs 18:9 "He also that is slothful in his work is brother to him that is a great waster."

Proverbs 19:15 "Slothfulness casteth into a deep sleep; and an idle soul shall suffer hunger."

Proverbs 19:24 "A slothful man hideth his hand in his bosom, and will not so much as bring it to his mouth again."

Proverbs 22:1 "The slothful man saith, There is a lion without, I shall be slain in the streets."

Proverbs 24:30 "I went by the field of the slothful, and by the

54

vineyard of the man void of understanding."

Proverbs 26:13 "The slothful man saith, There is a lion in the way; a lion is in the streets."

Proverbs 26:14 "As the door turneth upon his hinges, so doth the slothful upon his bed."

Proverbs 26:15 "The slothful hideth his hand in his bosom; it grieveth him to bring it again to his mouth."

[21]
Usury in Christendom: The Mortal Sin That Was and Now is Not by Michael Hoffman, 2013. Pages 163, 186.

History of Money and Usury In America
Part II
"Jefferson's Light"

By Daniel S. Krynicki
July 17, 2014
All Rights Reserved

*In **Part I** of this essay* a quotation was used on page 36 that purportedly originated with our third President Thomas Jefferson, *"I believe that banking institutions are more dangerous to our liberties than standing armies. If the American people ever allow private banks to control the issue of their currency, first by inflation, then by deflation, the banks and corporations that will grow up around the banks will deprive the people of all property - until their children wake-up homeless on the continent their fathers conquered. The issuing power should be taken from the banks and restored to the people, to whom it properly belongs."* This quotation can be found at the following url: http://foundersquotes.com/quotes/i-believe-that-banking-institutions-are-more-dangerous-to-our-liberties-than-standing-armies/#more-499 . It has not been an easy task to pinpoint a document or speech showing this quotation verbatim other than that Founder's quote web site. The people who created the Founders' Quote web site may have uncovered more of Jefferson's documents than what is readily available. It is reported on this web page that President Jefferson wrote this in the year 1802 in a letter or memo to his Treasury Secretary Albert Gallatin. Neither Paul Leicester Ford's nor Albert Ellery Bergh's

56

multi-volume sets *The Writings of Thomas Jefferson* [1] show this citation in any of his letters to Gallatin during the year 1802 ; nor does Paul Leicester Ford's *The Works of Thomas Jefferson, Federal Edition* [2] for the same year. Whether he wrote it before, during or after his presidency is unimportant. It could have been included in the minutes of a cabinet meeting or other recorded documents or speeches. If Jefferson did write at least something that closely parallels it, then use of the quote in *Part I* is validated. He did even better as we shall soon find out.

There was another book written in 1911 jointly by J.T. Holdsworth and Davis Rich Dewey, Volume IV called *Banking in United States Before Civil War* in which the two authors related the story that much of what passed with the First Bank of the US and even during Jefferson's presidency was done so in spite of his objections. Albert Gallatin, his treasury secretary, did much to temper his opposition to the US Bank charter. But we will find that his opinions were never deterred for a moment as we can find him repeating the same objections to the chair of the House Ways and Means, John Wayles Eppes in 1813.

Within the following pages, therefore, we shall show the proof of Thomas Jefferson's financial genius. We will also find even more information to validate that single quotation from the Founders' Quotes web site.

In three letters to John Eppes during 1813 Jefferson revealed in even greater detail - that his objectives were to end the bankers' authority to issue paper currency based on the amount of specie they held in deposits – and to end all fractional reserve lending (which is bank credit, or as Davis Rich Dewey wrote "book credit" in his *Financial History of the United States*).

This US Representative Eppes from Virginia was both Jefferson's nephew and son-in-law. These three letters were all written about four years after Jefferson vacated his office as the third president of the United States. Jefferson's daughter Mary or Maria Jefferson married Eppes who was elected to the Thirteenth

Congress (March 4, 1813 – March 4, 1815).

To this day it is believed that Ways and Means is singularly the most powerful committee in the House. But even though this is still believed to be true, Congress no longer exercises its Constitutional authority to issue our currency as did the Congress Eppes was a member of ; and therefore the people over at the Federal Reserve who create our currency have completely usurped this power from Congress. Instead, Congress now approves of interest bearing bond issues for which the **privately owned** international banking cartel known as the United States Federal Reserve issues our currency in return.

In the first letter dated June 24, 1813, Jefferson wrote that, *"This letter will be on politics only"*. Bear in mind that when anyone of that time period wrote on politics, the discussion may very well have been solely about economics. His only failure was the belief in Ben Franklin's philosophy that charging a reasonable interest rate on loans is both practical and beneficial and thus he perhaps never did realize that a usury free economic model would have proved itself to be a superior alternative. The full effect of employing a usury free economy would have completely driven the moneychangers out of the temple as Jefferson desired.

But instead of ever accomplishing this desired objective of his, he instead facilitated the moneychangers' foothold by endorsing Franklin's usury capitalism. 'A penny saved is a penny earned' is the type of nonsense promoted in Ben Franklin's philosophy. Incongruent maxims like this one gave rise to the capitalist maxims on the 'time value of money'. Equating labor with savings, therefore, gave rise to the theory that money should rather be classified as a fungible good upon which savings should collect interest. Jefferson noted in another letter that Franklin was the 'father of American philosophy' **[3]**. So we have Franklin and other descendants of the anti-usury Puritans to thank for shaping America into a non-Christian usury based capitalist nation.

Recall from *Part I* on page 17 there was discussion of another brilliant economist by the name of Gertrude Coogan [4]. She referenced Jefferson at length in her dissertation, so we can be comfortable that her entire model was based on analysis of Jefferson's and Franklin's philosophy. Though both Coogan and Jefferson had enough wisdom to identify money creation (as Coogan called it) or currency issue (as Jefferson called it) as a most important consideration in any economic model, neither spent time analyzing a system absent the usury as in a Christian model. Make no mistakes ; both currency creation and usury are equally important when considering long term long economic consequences. Jefferson's recommendation was to ultimately take away from private banks the authority to issue any currency, whether it was paper notes or credit. If he had been successful in keeping the issuance of our currency with Congress where it constitutionally belongs, usury in moneylending would eventually have been found to be completely unnecessary. This could be accomplished very easily while retaining free markets and civil liberties. Congress can even now institute a bureaucracy in which usury in all moneylending will be eliminated.

Jefferson also paid particularly close attention to accumulated debt of the nation over the long term. With a new federal institution issuing the currency to pay for the operational costs of government and lending usury free, national debt would no longer exist ; and all governmental operations and public infrastructure would be fully funded. According to Jefferson, passing on debt to succeeding generations for any reason is in effect a criminal offense in which the heirs become victims of their ancestors' indulgences. We shall cite Jefferson's comments on this also.

Let us begin, then, with some quotations out of Paul Leicester Ford's [5] *The Writings of Thomas Jefferson, Volume IX*, published in 1898, that contains Jefferson's three letters during 1813 to his son-in-law John Wayles Eppes who was, at the time, chair of the US House Ways and Means Committee:

On Debt - Page 389 Volume IX

"Never to borrow a dollar without laying a tax in the same instant for paying the interest annually, and the principal within a given term ;

"What is to hinder them from creating a perpetual debt? The laws of nature I answer. The earth belongs to the living, not to the dead.

"We may consider each generation as a distinct nation, with a right, by the will of its majority, to bind themselves, but none to bind the succeeding generation, more than the inhabitants of another country. Or the case may be likened to the ordinary one of a tenant for life, who may hypothecate the land for his debts, during the continuance of his usufruct ; but at his death, the reversioner (who is also for life only) receives it exonerated from all burthen. The period of a generation, or the term of its life, is determined by the laws of mortality.

"Are they (the descendants) *bound to acknowledge the debt, to consider the preceding generation as having had a right to eat up the whole soil of their country, in the course of a life, to alienate it from them (for it would be an alienation to the creditors,) and would they think themselves either legally or morally bound to give up their country and emigrate to another for subsistence?*

"And although, like some other natural rights, this has not yet entered into any declaration of rights, it is no less a law, and ought to be acted on by honest

governments.

"It is, at the same time, a salutary curb on the spirit of war and indebtment, which since the modern theory of the perpetuation of debt, has drenched the earth with blood, and crushed its inhabitants under burthens ever accumulating."

Imagine that ; Jefferson carefully explained over two hundred years ago how dangerous and amoral it is to accumulate a national debt and pass it on to succeeding generations. Notice how this mountain of national debt we have today that is ever increasing doesn't begin to fill the insatiable appetites usurers have to increase their holdings. In the year 2014 AD America's national debt stands at over $17 trillion. Out of the tax dollars collected by America's treasury department to pay its $3 Trillion budget, nearly $500 billion is used to pay just the annual interest. Meanwhile, the principal amount of this national debt is not going down ; it is increasing because the one half trillion we pay the bond holders as interest annually is not enough to reduce the principal.

It has been 201 years since Jefferson wrote those lines above. Was he prescient? No he wasn't ; he actually witnessed identical circumstances in his own lifetime. This is why he battled against Alexander Hamilton's insistence that Adam Smith's notion of public debt is a good thing.

What happened with the devout Christian George Washington? Did he believe Hamilton and Smith economics? Surely he must have missed Luke 6:35, Psalm 15:1-5 and Ezekiel 22:12 in his devotional Bible reading? Were there none of the early anti-usury Puritans remaining of those who settled early in Massachusetts Bay Colony during the seventeenth century?

This, though, is only the beginning in Jefferson's three

long letters to the Chair of the House Ways and Means Committee, his own son-in-law. Thus far in the foregoing excerpts he has only discussed debt. Issuance of the currency we shall see is a real prize that was served up to the moneylenders on December 23, 1913. A corrupt Congress and an idiot president knew next to nothing about finance and only the whitewashed parts of American History. This Woodrow Wilson also happened to be the 13th President of Princeton University.

On Issuing Paper Currency

Before Jefferson's next set of quotes is reprinted herein, a cautionary note is in order: In our present usury capitalist system, bankers employ torturously complex devices as tools for attaining their objectives. Two hundred years ago such complexity was also employed, but the devices used as tools differed in some ways. Learning even a little about these differences will go a long way in understanding that nothing at all has changed in the bankers' objectives across these two hundred years. The bankers have always rigged the system for their own benefit to the detriment of their customers and the national economy.

Various instruments in current use are:
1. Private Currency Issue (Federal Reserve Notes) in exchange for Treasury Bonds issued by the Treasury Department.
2. Bank Credit
   a) Mortgages
      i) Fixed Rate
      ii) Adjustable Rate
   b) Auto Loans
   c) Credit Cards
3. Bundling and Selling of Loan Packages into Leveraged Insurance Contracts (A high stakes betting game). [6]

a) Credit Default Swaps
b) Derivatives

The third category is a more exotic and highly complex category that began to emerge during the mid-1980s and soared after Glass-Steagall was partially dismantled in bipartisan fashion near the end of William Clinton's second term. It is known as the Financial Services Modernization Act of 1999.

During Jefferson's era, the instruments of bankers' deceit are more commonly known, but not less complex in operation and just as destructive economically to the national welfare. They are as follows:

1. Bills of Credit emissions as loans of legal tender at interest to citizens at large by the First Bank of the United States.
2. Book credit by private banks as loans at interest to citizens at large.
3. Privately issued bank paper notes as loans and redeemable in specie. These were not legal tender as the Bills of Credit were.

Here now are excerpts beginning on page 392
Of Paul Ford's Volume IX:

(As in Chapter 1 where long quotations by Davis Rich Dewey and others were used, the underlining was not in the original text. The underlining and bold were added here for emphasis so that the reader can easily single out the details we need to understand.)

"But this, the only resource which the government could command with certainty, the States have unfortunately fooled away, nay corruptly alienated to swindlers and shavers, under the cover of private banks. Say, too, as an additional evil, that the disposal funds of individuals, to this great amount, have thus been withdrawn from improvement and useful enterprise, and employed in the

useless, usurious and demoralizing practices of bank *directors and their accomplices.* In the war of 1755, our State (Virginia) *availed itself of this fund by issuing a* *paper money, bottomed on a specific tax for its* *redemption, and, to insure its credit, bearing an interest* *of five percent. Within a very short time, not a bill of* *this emission was to be found in circulation. It was* *locked up in the chests of executors, guardians, widows,* *farmers, &c.* We then issued bills bottomed on a *redeeming tax, but bearing no interest. These were* *readily received, and never depreciated a single* *farthing. In the revolutionary war, the old Congress* *and the States issued bills without interest and without* *tax. They occupied the channels of circulation very* *freely, til those channels were overflowed by an excess* *beyond all the calls of circulation. But although we* *have so improvidently suffered the field of circulating* *medium to be filched from us by private individuals,*

Excerpts from page 393 Volume IX:

"would not take them in preference to the bank paper *now afloat, on a principle of patriotism as well as* *interest ; and they would be withdrawn from circulation* *into private hoards to a considerable amount. Their* *credit once established, others might be emitted,* *bottomed also on a tax, but not bearing interest ; and if* *ever their credit faltered, open public loans, on which* *these bills alone should be received as specie.*

"It is not easy to estimate the obstacles which, in the

beginning we should encounter in ousting the banks from their possession of the circulation ; but a steady and judicious alternation of emissions and loans, would reduce them in time. But while this is going on, another measure should be pressed, to <u>recover ultimately our right to the circulation</u>. The States should be applied to, to transfer the right of issuing circulating paper to Congress exclusively, in perpetuum if possible, but during the war at least, with a saving of charter rights.
"Congress would, of course, begin by obliging unchartered banks to wind up their affairs within a short time, and the others as their charters expired, forbidding the subsequent circulation of their paper.
"It would be in their power, too, to <u>curtail those banks to the amount of their actual specie</u>, by gathering up their paper and running it constantly on them. <u>The national paper might thus take place even in the non-complying States</u>. In this way, I am not without a hope, that this great, this sole resource for loans in an agricultural country, might yet be recovered for the use of the nation during war ; and, <u>if obtained in perpetuum</u>, it would always be sufficient to carry us through any war,"

Following here now is a single sentence in this letter from Jefferson to Eppes that not only embodies the philosophy of Benjamin Franklin, but also formed the belief upon which Gertrude Coogan allowed as the one serious flaw in her dissertation. Whether or not Ms. Coogan took notice of the superior usury free Mosaic model in any subsequent writing

we cannot know.   If she published anything else, it is
overshadowed by her fame from *Money Creators* and is probably
not available commercially.

From page 394 Volume IX:
*"No one has a natural right to the trade of a money
lender, but he who has the money to lend."*

Well, President Jefferson, how then can Congress emit
'bills of credit' (create new money) and then charge interest for
the created legal tender's use, especially if, as you wrote, the
national credit belongs to the people? This is the point at which
this writer began to see that both Jefferson and Franklin had to
have a sub-conscious double-mindedness unknowingly deep-
rooted into their ethos. Make no mistake, they were dealing all
the time with hucksters, shysters, swindlers, shavers, sophists and
con artists.   They may not have seen the inherent deception
involved in charging interest on loans for which new money
needed to be created for every loan contract. In effect, they were
merely imitating the moneylender's tradecraft ; that is, imitating
what they thought was a perfectly reasonable method of lending
of the nation's assets to raise money for the expenditures of
legitimate government. They were trying to accomplish all this in
a corrupt world. Jesus called it the unrighteousness mammon.

What was really needed then, and still is, would be
passage into law of what Jefferson's heartfelt inclination was as it
was poured out in his letter to his son-in-law Senator Eppes,
*"transfer the right of issuing circulating paper to
Congress exclusively, in perpetuum"*. This certainly would
have provided our fledgling nation with a better opportunity for
economic success. There were real patriots back then who would
have used this power to 'promote the general welfare'. But at the
same time, they would also have only implemented one third of

the needed solution. What need is there for usury if Congress has the exclusive authority to issue the currency? If they are the only body with authority to issue currency, they should also form an institution of their own to have sole authority to issue credit along with currency. If they pay for all of Government's expenditures out of this currency and credit creating power, they could also lend of this credit to the people without charging interest. What need therefore is there for any but one tax to balance the money supply with the GDP? How did Howard Rand put it? "We will out capital capitalism" with usury outlawed!

With all who are presently issuing bank credit, exactly who or what institution with authority is at the helm regulating the money supply to be in balance with the GDP? There isn't one except the oversight of the privately owned, run by criminals, Federal Reserve. Constitutionally, oversight is the responsibility and authority of Congress, not a Treasury Department that operates in the Executive branch. But does it matter which has oversight if a privately owned criminal-banking cartel issues the nation's currency and credit? As the result of this power that our beltway harlequins ceded to them, they also control all three branches of our federal government. No one except large multinational corporations along with the banking cartels can afford the high price involved in the electoral process. The people now have next to nothing in the way of representation because only high finance, a few billionaires and the corporatocracy have access to huge volumes of capital.

With usury being charged for every dollar in circulation except the small coins, the entire system is deflationary ; so much so that more credit must be issued just to pay the interest due. This means the *money supply* is ever expanding (inflating) in order to pay for interest ; while at the same time it is in a continuously deflationary process. Jefferson explained it in his wheat analogy: the price of a bushel doubled when the money supply expanded by a factor of ten. The farmer therefore lost to the monetary inflation resulting from the ten notes to one in specie circulating. And there was no law restricting the amount of leveraging bankers were allowed in 1813. Coogan reported it was thirty-three to one on time deposits after the Federal Reserve Act was passed. It's so mind boggling that it can be described as somewhat of a conundrum, namely, a riddle that cannot be solved by anything on the table except the one put into writing 3,500 years ago by Moses. How many among the educated have vision based on the simplest of all solutions? It has been on the books for three and a half millennia.

How many among us have observed a joint hearing of Congress in which the chairperson of the **Fed** slyly gave no answers to the hearing committee? Hubris from the agents of the **Fed** is at an all time high. They are not forthright with any of their answers. They must necessarily be this way so that the general public will have no inclination, no clue as to what is really happening. Jefferson's explanation of the same phenomenon was recorded for us similarly in Volume IX of Paul Ford's *The Writings of Thomas Jefferson*:

Page 394 Volume IX:

"Private fortunes, in the present state of our circulation, are at the mercy of those self-created money lenders, and are prostrated by the floods of nominal money with which their avarice deluges us. He who lent his money to the public or to an individual, before the institution of the United States Bank, twenty years ago, when wheat was well sold at a dollar the bushel, and receives now his nominal sum when it sells at two dollars, is cheated of half his fortune ; and by whom? By the banks, which since that, have thrown into circulation ten dollars of their nominal money where was one at that time."

In his second letter to Eppes that year, dated September 11, 1813, Jefferson picked up where he left off with bank paper. At that time bank paper accomplished the same effects as bank credit and as US Treasury Bonds do today with Federal Reserve Notes. So we learn from this that private banks not only had book credit operating during Jefferson's epoch ; they also issued bank paper, both of which served as money in the currency stream ; neither of which was legal tender as the 'bills of credit' issued by the Bank of the United States were.

Page 399 Volume IX:

"The question will be asked and ought to be looked at, what is to be the resource if loans cannot be obtained? There is but one, 'Carthato delenda est'. <u>*Bank paper*</u> <u>*must be suppressed, and the circulating medium must be*</u> <u>*restored to the nation to whom it belongs*</u>*. It is the only fund on which they can rely for loans ; it is the only resource which can never fail them, and it is an abundant one for every necessary purpose.* <u>*Treasury*</u> <u>*bills, bottomed on taxes, bearing or not bearing interest,*</u> <u>*as may be found necessary, thrown into circulation will*</u> <u>*take the place of so much gold and silver, which last,*</u> <u>*when crowded, will find an efflux into other countries,*</u> <u>*and thus keep the quantum of medium at its salutary*</u> <u>*level*</u>*. Let banks continue if they please, but let them discount for cash alone or for treasury notes.*

Here Jefferson injects a Latin phrase from the Punic Wars as a metaphor for the bankers. These wars were waged between Rome and Carthage over usury. He fully understood that there was an ongoing battle between usury banking and 'the people'. But he only discovered one third of the needed solution, namely that treasury 'bills' (or notes) should be issued federally, not privately. Along with this, he noted that they needed to suppress 'bank paper' (bank notes). *(Carthage must be destroyed!)* Notice here that he did not yet mention 'bank' or 'book' credit. This also floods the currency stream with interest bearing debt, something that is deflationary. So bank paper and book credit therefore constituted two thirds of the problem. The other third is usury.

In the following excerpt pages (402, 403, 404) Jefferson continued with his disapprobation of bank paper:

Page 402 Volume IX:

"My original disapprobation of banks circulating paper is not unknown, nor have I since observed any effects either on the morals or fortunes of our citizens, which are any counterbalance for the public evils produced ; and a thorough conviction that, if this war continues, that circulation must be suppressed, or the government shaken to its foundation by the weight of taxes, and impracticability to raise funds on them, renders duty to that paramount to the love of ease and quiet.

Page 403:

(From a letter he received from Mr. Law on the establishment of a national bank and issuing treasury notes)
"This paper contains two propositions ; the one for issuing treasury notes, bearing interest, and to be circulated as money ; the other for the establishment of a national bank.
"Neither Congress nor the states having any power of

interference in its administration.

Page 404:

"2. They authorize this bank to throw into circulation ninety millions of dollars, (three times the capital.) which increases our circulating medium fifty perc., depreciates proportionably the present value of a dollar, and raises the price of all future purchases in the same proportion.

"4. no one has a right ever to see their books, or to ask a question, they may choose their time for running away, after adding to their booty the proceeds of as much of their own notes as they shall be able to throw into circulation.

*"5. Whereupon this **bank oligarchy** or monarchy enters the field with ninety millions of dollars, **to direct on our politics**, and into what scale it will be thrown, we have had abundant experience.*

*"6. This state of things is to be fastened on us, without the power of **relief**, for forty or fifty years.*

"7. But the great and national advantage is to be the relief of the present scarcity of money, which is produced and proved by."

Relief? What sort of relief have the bankers provided for America. As it was when Jefferson lived, so it still is today as Rev. Charles Coughlin chimed during the 1930s, *"Relief That Fails to Relieve"*! [7] In this set of consecutive excerpts Jefferson correctly identified banks circulating their own paper notes in the currency stream as a serious problem. These complaints Jefferson enumerated should also have been forthcoming from those who cross-examined cryptic Ben Shalom Bernanke at Congressional hearings. In his replies to the Congressional questioners 'Helicopter Ben' kept a dead calm straight face with every phony answer he gave. The only congressman complaining (Ron Paul) in recent memory in our government has retired from office. He may very well have fully understood that the banking community is bilking us. So his posturing was absolutely justified. But the solution he advocated is the brainchild of Ludwig von Mises, the Austrian school founder. It too is pro-usury and anti-Christian.

There was another congressman from Texas who retired probably during the 1980s who also complained about the **Fed** as much as Ron Paul did. His name was Henry Gonzales from Texas. But where are any like them now? Where are the complainers demanding answers from the criminal **Fed** cartel? Even Ron Paul's son Senator Rand Paul makes very little noise about the banking system. And don't hold your breath waiting for a hue and cry from anyone in the beltway. Wall Street owns it. In fact, even all the complainers there never said anything against usury. Even the pulpits are silent.

Ron Paul leaned toward going back to a gold standard, which is precisely what early America was on when the banking shavers and connivers bilked every dollar they could out of our young republic. Yes that's right ; the monetary reformers over at the von Mises Institute, the Austrian school of economics, would have us go back to the same system that already proved itself useful only at being confiscatory of people's labor and property as well as plaguing the people with price inflation as evidenced from the legacy of writings that Jefferson left with us. And instead of looking at the only solution that could possibly end economic tyranny, Jefferson instead leaned to liking only gold as money, just like Ron Paul and the Austrian schoolers. At the same time he approved of interest on loans of paper money that was created out of nothing. How much more double-minded can one get?

72

It wouldn't be fair for any of us to say there weren't founders who objected to a non-Christian economic platform. If there were though, we could probably count them with ten fingers.

In Jefferson's defense though, at various points throughout these three letters, Jefferson explained carefully how important it was for the US Congress to have the exclusive authority to issue the nation's currency. But this advocacy for federal authority came from the man who wrote that Alexander Hamilton was the 'Colossus of Federalism' in 1795 **[8]**. Here he had another double-minded attitude. Doesn't this seem a bit ironic? How did President Jefferson, four years after leaving the office of President, suggest that elected officials should become involved at the federal level in solving the swindling and shaving bankers were doing to the people? Why the patriotism and nationalism for a government that did nothing at all to provide the cure for diseases that they ably identified in the Unanimous Declaration - tyranny, oppressive taxation and despotism? The only one they missed was *economic oppression*. A usury laden, debt based monetary system will always lead to *economic oppression*. None of these ills can be solved until an honest monetary system is institutionalized in which usury is forever prohibited on loans of money.

Fractional Reserve Banking
We shall now look a little at what can be identified in modern terms as fractional reserve banking. Jefferson ably described it. And while explaining it, he also described meticulously to us how these banking practices were prevalent during the epoch in which he lived. We should also notice that such practices were commonly used dating back even further than the founding of the Bank of England in 1694. In his *Usury in Christendom*, **[9]** Michael Hoffman described the Three for One Monte. This was a 15th century Florentine banking practice prior

to Renaissance times that also was a form of fractional reserve banking.

It's far more sophisticated today. All a bank needs now is paperwork showing the borrower has the ability to pay on a loan and the certificate of collateral on the property the borrower is paying for. Can it really be described as a loan? Just as with Treasury Bonds this security is all banks need to create new money as credit. If there is such a thing as a reserve requirement today, we can get a lesson on this topic from CR Dickey and Gertrude Coogan in [*Is Economic Ruin Inevitable?*] 1949, Destiny Publishers [10], when they were lying to us saying gold actually backed the money they were issuing as book credit and notes. And since 1968, there has not even been the illusion of fractional reserve lending when 'PAYABLE TO THE BEARER ON DEMAND' was removed from Federal Reserve Notes.

There is therefore no such thing as the Federal Deposit Insurance Corporation. It certainly is a fiction. All our deposits are fully insured by Helicopter Bernanke ; or is it Janet Yellen now? But insure it they will only if they decide to. They may or may not, if and whenever they decide to. All Yellen needs to do is print a few more paper dollars or issue cyberspace credit to banks that have a run. This writer once read (around 2008) in the WSJ that the **Fed** can issue all the currency it wants to. They will issue all the dollars they need to keep the system solvent if and when it will benefit them. In fact, across the past six years, the Federal Reserve has even issued billions in American currency to bail out private banks situated in New York City with no strings attached. They called it "Quantitative Easing" ; and they did it several times.

During the same period of time, millions of homeowners lost their homes through foreclosure because also, at the beginning of this same period, the bankers deliberately shrunk credit emissions to businesses. The consequences of this resulted in millions laid off from their jobs. There was no quantitative easing given freely to home mortgagees from the private Fed to relieve stress as was given freely to more than several Wall Street banking houses.

Oh, the federal government, through one of their formerly owned mortgage corporations like Fannie Mae perhaps, allowed a program of mortgage restructuring for distressed homeowners in 2008 to lower their interest rates. But five years hence from then - which is now - the mortgage rates are scheduled to be reset back to their original rate. Homeowners are now facing mortgage payments of fifty to one-hundred dollars more per month than what their restructured rate was beginning five years ago. Those who were allowed to restructure in the year 2009 will experience the same rate increase five years after their restructuring. Thank you federal government for giving five years of relief to homeowners with their mortgage payments while billions were given gratis to Wall Street international banks whose executives never even skipped a beat with their high salaries and bonuses. Either strip away from them the power to create money along with the ability to charge usury, or remain forever in debt bondage to them. All usury in moneylending must be prohibited.

Consider something Davis Dewey reported in his **Financial History of the United States**: During the Civil War Salmon P. Chase explained the results of allowing usury ; but he did not comprehend why this is so, *"he did call attention to the inconveniences and hazards of the issue of United States notes, possibly ending in the 'immeasurable evils of dishonest public faith and national bankruptcy'."* (Dewey Pages 279-283) Have the immeasurable evils ever been mitigated by allowing private banks to create our currency and credit? The problem is usury, not government created fiat money.

We will here get back to the main person in our study with a final set of excerpts in which Jefferson provided us with a detailed explanation of 'quantitative easing' using his two hundred year old terminology.

From Paul Ford Volume IX Page 414:

"That ordinary price has now doubled with us, and more than doubled in England: and although a part of this augmentation may proceed from the war demand, yet from the extraordinary nominal rise in the prices of land and labor here, both of which have nearly doubled in that period, *and are still rising with every new bank, it is evident that were a general peace to take place to-morrow, and time allowed for the re-establishment of commerce, justice, and order,* we could not afford to raise wheat for much less than two dollars.

"It is said that our paper is as good as silver, because we may have silver for it at the bank where it issues. This is not true. *One, two, or three persons might have it; but a* general application would soon exhaust their vaults, and leave a ruinous proportion of their paper in its intrinsic worthless form. *It is a fallacious pretence, for another reason. The inhabitants of the banking cities might obtain cash for their paper, as far as the cash of the vaults would hold out, but distance puts it out of the power of the country to do this.* A farmer having a note of Boston or Charleston bank, distant hundreds of miles, has no means of calling for the cash. *And while these calls are impracticable for the country, the banks have no fear of their being made from the towns ; because their inhabitants are mostly on their books, and there on sufferance only, and during good*

76

behavior.

"Owing to the support its credit receives from the <u>small</u> <u>reservoirs of specie in the vaults or the banks, it is</u> <u>impossible to say at what point their notes will stop</u>. Nothing is necessary to effect but a general alarm ; and that may take place whenever the public shall begin to reflect on, and perceive the impossibility that the banks should repay this sum.

Page 415:

"The inhabitants of the banking towns will get what is in the vaults, until a few banks declare their insolvency ; when, the general crush becoming evident, the others will withdraw even the cash they have, declare their bankruptcy at once, <u>and leave an empty house and</u> <u>empty coffers for the holders of their notes.</u> <u>In this</u> <u>scramble of creditors, the country gets nothing, the</u> <u>towns but little.</u> What are they to do? Bring suits? A million of creditors bring a million of suits against John Nokes and Robert Styles, wheresoever to be found? <u>All</u> <u>Nonsense.</u> <u>The loss is total.</u> <u>And a sum is thus swindled</u> <u>from our citizens</u>, of seven times the amount of the real debt, and <u>four times that of the fictitious one of the</u> <u>United States</u>, at the close of the war.

"<u>It is time, then, for the public functionaries to look to</u> <u>this</u>.

"in their hands, it will continue to go on from bad to worse, until the catastrophe overwhelms us.

"Any single State, even if no other should come into the

measure, would find its interest in arresting foreign bank paper immediately, and its own by degrees.

Page 416:

"Should the greater part of the States concede, as is expected, their power over banks to Congress, besides insuring their own safety, the paper of the non-conceding States might be so checked and circumscribed, by prohibiting its receipt in any of the conceding States, and even in the non-conceding as to duties, taxes, judgments, or other demands of the United States, or of the citizens of other States, that it would soon die of itself, and the medium of gold and silver be universally restored. This is what ought to be done. But it will not be done, Carthago non delibitur. The overbearing clamor of merchants, speculators, and projectors, will drive us before them with our eyes open, until, as in under the Mississippi bubble, our citizens will be overtaken by the crush of this baseless fabric, without other satisfaction than that of execrations on the heads of those functionaries, who from ignorance, pusillanimity or corruption, have betrayed the fruits of their industry into the hands of projectors and swindlers.

"When I speak comparatively of the paper emissions of the old Congress and the present banks, let it not be imagined that I cover them under the same mantle. The object of the former was a holy one ; for if ever there was a holy war, it was that which saved our liberties

and gave us independence. The object of the latter, is to enrich swindlers at the expense of the honest and industrious part of the nation."

So there we have it, excerpts from Jefferson's letters to Eppes in 1813, albeit not in the same terminology we in the present day are accustomed to when discussing economics. So we must proceed slowly and deliberately so that misunderstandings shall be avoided.

In these three letters to his son-in-law, US Representative Eppes from Virginia, Jefferson wrote that the only way to stop the subterfuge and conniving that results from bank paper and bank credit is to federalize all of it. But even at this stage of his life he still didn't grasp that even federalized systems like this will allow transfer of capital to officials (usurpers and embezzlers) when usury is allowed. Why is this so? Let us stop here and take notice of all the principal parties involved in the usury scheme two hundred years ago.

Jefferson's treasury secretary Albert Gallatin was opposed to the 'colossus of federalism' Alexander Hamilton and his First Bank of the United States during the 1790s. But when he came to power himself as treasury secretary in 1801, he kept all the main parts thus supporting the US Bank that other Jeffersonians vehemently opposed.

But notice also that Albert Gallatin's son James Gallatin was the agent from the New York banks sent as the messenger to negotiate with Civil War treasury secretary Salmon P. Chase about the 'Greenbacks' that were being issued to pay for public dues in prosecution of the war. This James Gallatin succeeded his father Albert as the President of the Gallatin National Bank in 1839. It's a shame to find out that even a presidential administration headed by a Thomas Jefferson wound up victim to the infiltration of swindlers and shavers. Bankers like Albert and

James Gallatin attached themselves as parasites to our young republic as soon as it was born.

Dr. Franklin must have convinced Jefferson earlier on in his life that moderate interest rates on loans are not harmful to the economy. It is indeed baffling how such a brilliant mind should miss that when businesses, merchants, professionals and laborers borrow at interest to retail whatever it is they sell, all the interest they pay to lenders must be obtained from the prices of their goods and services, as does all the interest they must have paid for their student loans before they entered the work force. And even if student loans were not a big issue two hundred years ago, they certainly are today. There is no other way for people to acquire the interest for their loans except to include in their fees and prices the amount that is needed to pay the interest.

To this day, only a handful in alternative media teaches that usury is harmful. And because there is this mirage of federal money creation through the Federal Reserve, some people think that local currencies must at all costs be the objective. Jefferson had some light ; but it was dimmed by his acceptance that usury is not amoral.

What should we notice from this last set of excerpts that Jefferson wrote? There are some key points we should compare with present times to see if the **Federal Reserve System** is actually performing its mission as originally chartered. We can also ask if there exists such a thing as a privately owned banking system that will not swindle people out of their honestly obtained earnings.

In the part of the excerpts identified as **From Page 414** of Ford's Volume IX and **From Page 415**, it is easily seen that in this earliest period during the history of the United States under the Constitution, the people were afflicted with price inflation in the same way we now experience it. We labor for a lifetime and save for our old age only to have what we saved stolen by helicopter pilots like Janet Yellen and Ben Bernanke. Names mean little here ; all their predecessors are as guilty as the two mentioned, all the way back to Colonial times. In 1813 private banks issued both bank notes redeemable for specie and book credit thus flooding the money supply that was already awash with federally issued legal tender 'bills of credit'.

On **Page 414** Jefferson also noted that foreign bank paper was circulating which assuredly made even worse the price inflation domestic bankers caused. These periods of booms evidenced by price inflation throughout our history have unfailingly always been followed by bust cycles known as panics and recessions.

In his book ***End the Fed***, Ron Paul identified on page twenty-seven just about every panic and recession America experienced during the 20th century. Gertrude Coogan [4] in her ***Money Creators*** identified other panics during the latter half 19th century and early 20th century. We have here also the third President of the United States writing about exactly the same kind of price inflation and bust cycles in a long letter to the Chair of House Ways and Means in 1813. These bust cycles are engineered conditions moneychangers are able to easily implement as a result of private money creation at interest. The top echelon in banking is patient to watch for the results their actions are designed to cause. The bankers gobble up choice assets during the bust cycles

As we move along through this set of excerpts, we will find words and certain phrases that are not normally used in the present day as Jefferson used them. When Jefferson wrote *"a general application would soon exhaust their vaults"*, he referred to a run on the bank in which depositors who wanted to redeem their dollars for specie all came in at once with paper currency they had in their pockets. This is just the obviously recognizable aspect of a run on the bank that holds gold in reserve to purportedly back the paper notes they issued.

In 1933 a bank run occurred in America at the height of the second wave of the Great Depression. The solution Congress passed in response to it was known as the 'Bank Holiday' or "Emergency Banking Act" for short. The actual title was Emergency Banking Relief Act. [11] It became the law of the land after Congress held a joint session here in America three days after FDR declared a bank holiday. When the banks refused to open their doors, the people soon found out just whom the money and gold banks had on deposit belonged to. It wound up in the pockets of the shavers and swindlers, in other words in the bankers' pockets, same as it did during Jefferson's epoch ; or could we still be in the same banking epoch?

We also have here examples from two hundred years ago explained by a near genius about how sly and underhanded bankers were at practicing the art of money creation. With gold backed currency, money creation is supposed to be contingent on a ratio between the amount of paper currency a bank issues and the amount of specie the bank has either on deposit or in its vault. Here, in some of Jefferson's lines shown on page 76 (Ford's Vol. IX page 414), we find they wrote bank notes for which they had nothing in their vaults - *"Owing to the support its credit receives from the small reservoirs of specie in the vaults or the banks, it is impossible to say at what point their notes will stop."* Does this mean fractional reserve banking or doesn't it? Jefferson made no mention of a specific ratio between the private paper currency issue and the specie held by the bank as the collateral that was supposed to back the currency. He also explained that it was impossible to say at what point their notes would stop. In other words, there was no law written to limit the ratio of leveraging allowed to the bankers. It was obvious to Jefferson that they would lend anything that was asked of them, if book credit or privately issued notes can be called lending. Could we honestly believe they imparted something in the loan process that they actually held in their possession? They do collect usury for this money they did not have to lend. Review Jefferson's sentence carefully. Cursory reading of these historical documents does not help readers to totally comprehend such a slick subject as economics. It takes mental acuity and focus to fully grasp what the street-smart swindlers and shavers are peddling at any given moment.

So here it is two hundred years later and the same scenario is still being played out over and over. One would think everything that's going on is normal by observing newscasts and reading newspapers. Why is this? Because the bootlicker presstitutes do not report these facts ; they are totally controlled by the moneyed elite.

And just how complicit or guilty are the institutions of higher learning for not actively expounding on the highly animated disputes that existed between the bankers and American elected officials during Colonial period, Continental Congress, the early Constitutional Republic and the Civil War period. We really need to dig out obscure financial history books [12] for a good look at these financial conflicts. Much occurred after America's founding ; and enough truth was written about what transpired in sufficient detail so that the only excuse Americans have for not taking notice from alarms such as Jefferson's is cultivated ignorance by an inordinate amount of bread and circus along with the academics not fulfilling their responsibilities and a sycophant press.

A wise electrician once reminded me that the Lord has yet reserved for Himself seven thousand who have not bowed to Baal. (Romans 11:4, I Kings 19:18.) People like him are those who search the Scriptures daily to verify whether or not their paths will stay on the straight and narrow. Remember, broad is the path that leads to destruction. Entrance in is only allowed at the straight gate. How do people not perceive that, with having the blessing of free will, all must be allowed to choose between right and wrong? God's people must necessarily live in this world of choice in order to accumulate the wisdom and knowledge that it will take to become a permanent member in Christ's emerging kingdom.

The Tea Party and Dr. David Brat

As a corollary to this *Part II*, and because John Wayles Eppes was a member of the House and chaired Ways and Means, it would also be good to look into the state of affairs in our present US Congress. To say the least, the situation looks bleak. Even those in Congress who have some sort of vision in which they propose to lead us out of the present state of decline in our republic, none look at a solution in which the usury beast's head is cut off. None dare suggest that usury on simple loans be abolished; none dare suggest that usury free national credit belongs to the people as Jefferson did, that establishment of a national credit agency would not be an insurmountable task, or even not an unconstitutional federal institution. Look what FDR accomplished with a nationally administered Social Security System. But what do these lawyers and PhDs in Congress offer us today? Every essay they write, every word they issue out of their mouths in no way ever suggests doing away with usury on simple loans as well as doing away with private creation of money and credit. Yet at the founding of this nation, it was first and foremost in all their minds, as Franklin and Jefferson promoted, to issue their own currency.

So let us start here with a recent Republican primary winner for the US House whose name is David Brat, PhD.

It's sad to see that modern economists with a PhD completely circumnavigate around the ancient model committed into writing by the ancient Israelites ; they never give it any serious consideration. Worse than that, some quotations from an essay by Dr. Brat will demonstrate convincingly and exactly that rather than follow the teachings of Christ, he has chosen to teach,

84

as a professor, along that broad road that leads to destruction. In most every quotation from him that is included further on herein, it shows that his main concern is simply with economics ; and his referencing from the Bible is only the result of his superficial understanding of it or what his heretic friends at the Calvinist seminary provide to him. He never includes in his discussion how a usury free system of credit, capitalist at its core – but without interest on all simple loan contracts, would be superior to anything taught today in higher education. If Dr. Brat is an example of what our educational system has produced to become teachers, we can expect only the worst of conditions to prevail.

Professor David Brat, PhD

Already visible are the many living in this nation today who have very little in the way of material possessions ; and even the resources they are able to scramble for are exploited and usurped by the few who live their lives of comfort and ease. It takes us straight into the core of the Christian belief from which we can recall vividly the story Jesus told about the poor beggar Lazarus and the rich man. Has the Tea Party Republican candidate from Virginia thoroughly read the New Testament with an open heart? After reading some from one of his essays, the reader should be convinced he has not.

He is now running for a congressional seat in Virginia after recently winning a primary election upsetting an entrenched Republican Congressman by the name of Eric Cantor. Mr. Brat chairs the Department of Economics and Business at Randolph-Macon College. From his *[God and Advanced Mammon---Can Theological Types Handle Usury and Capitalism?]* essay of

April 1, 2011 we find him supporting Adam Smith and Ayn Rand. We must distinguish here that by supporting Smith's and Ayn Rand's theories he is actually in favor of debt/usury based capitalism. None of the economists like him ever suggest that there could exist a non-usurious form of capitalism, nor does he offer such an alternative study in his paper. Perhaps because this alternative is never considered in the higher learning institutions, these brilliant professors haven't yet attained the real vision embodied in Mosaic capitalism. They ignore it as a subject because they commonly accept all of Dr. Franklin's philosophy ; and true to form as politicians they defend it zealously without considering the nasty side effects of ever increasing price inflation with the poor left in the ditch never even able to afford bare necessities such as food, shelter, clothing or quality medical care. Sure, the corporate capitalists have brought in foreign goods into America, the costs of which are so low they are able to obtain enough food for a spartan diet and clothing. But local housing only becomes affordable through federal subsidies or by living in blighted areas where millions and millions of foreclosures and vacated homes exist. We know them today as ghetto slums that are populated primarily by squatters.

A bare outline of a usury free alternative modernized capitalist system was provided for the reader in *Part I* of this paper. 3,500 years ago Moses gave us the Lord's ancient outline of the same system. Brat explores nothing similar, even though his advanced degree designates him as expert in all things economic.

Mr. Brat begins his paper with the heading **"Category Errors—We Think Usury is Bad"**. Perhaps, at some level and in a few ways, usury is not bad. As noted in *Part I* of this essay, there certainly exists more than one form of loan contract, some for which the lender puts up absolutely nothing at risk as a borrower does. This is bank credit that operates in the currency stream as money. But if we would "Lend, asking for nothing in return" on simple loan contracts as Jesus taught us in Luke 6:35 and out of our federal institution known as the National Credit Agency, the moneylenders would then vacate the temple of their own volition. Would prices on retail goods and services go down as a result of this? Usury would be an absent cost in all prices. The moneychangers would then need to learn a new skill or continue in the new federal monetary authority as accountants or clerks to administer the funding of government and usury free lending.

Before we show a few more of his quotations, we should first ask if Dr. Brat grew up in an area that was primarily occupied by the labor class, be it skilled, manual, clerical or otherwise. Most of these occupations bring in earnings at nearly the same levels. Was he able to visibly watch his neighborhood deteriorate when millions of jobs were lost across the past 40-year period as the corporatocracy offshored their manufacturing facilities into slave labor class nations? All of these job losses to even the last person here in America were a shock to families who could not find replacement jobs with comparable wage scales. Many were forced to flip burgers at fast food restaurants. Others, when their jobless benefits ran out, as skilled in some tradecraft, refused to work for minimum wage and thereby became a permanent fixture in the welfare system ; and some are now operating strictly for cash in the underground economy. Was Dr. Brat insulated from this decline in the American labor force? Have the princes of industry suffered ill effects monetarily as labor has suffered? The opposite is true. The princes of industry have used this decline to neutralize any effectiveness unions have had in the past at bringing American labor into a respectable standard of living.

Mr. Brat asks, *"Do we have the right to coerce our fellow citizens to act in ways that follow our Christian ethical beliefs?"* Absolutely not! But we should ask him first:

How can you claim 'our Christian ethical beliefs' when you ignore the command of Jesus in Luke 6:35 and in other Scriptural passages like Leviticus 25, Deuteronomy 15, Psalm 15, Ezekiel 18 and Ezekiel 22 where all domestic usury is prohibited? You cannot claim to be a Christian and write as such without first exhausting every jot and tittle in the Christian Bible.

More Quotations from Dr. Brat

"The Bible is clear that usury should not be practiced in small religious communities where loans involving the deep familial bond of brothers and sisters occur, especially poor brothers and sisters. It is less clear on usury in general, but it is safe to say that a tension exists."

"Money changers eventually began keeping deposits for various clients, so that when two clients made an exchange, all the money changers had to do was credit one account and subtract from the other. Simple arithmetic had replaced a risky and cumbersome movement of coins."

"At some point, though, the old ban on usury started to stick out like a sore thumb. It slowly dawned on people that money lent for capital was different from money lent to a poor neighbor out of need. When banks charge interest on a loan.....they're charging for something. By lending money, for instance, the bank is forgoing other opportunities to use the money, and it is taking a risk in lending the money in the first place."

"For the economist, there is no unjust charge. There is

no exploitation. Why? Because economists do not do ethics, by definition. We do social science. The good news here is that if you ever hear an economist giving ethical advice, you should not give that advice much attention. Economists are here to describe the world as it is, not as it should be. In economics, there can be no price too high, because if a product sells at a high price, then clearly it was not too high."

These four are only a few of his misconceptions on reality that we will attend to here.

Dr. Brat's first in this set of quotes wasn't even thought through either before he wrote it or after. *"The Bible is clear that usury should not be practiced in small religious communities where loans involving the deep familial bond of brothers and sisters occur, especially poor brothers and sisters. It is less clear on usury in general, but it is safe to say that a tension exists."*

This is evidence that Dr. Brat's observations in Leviticus 25 are the result of, at best, cursory reading. Religious life had absolutely nothing to do with the Mosaic Law as given to the Ancient Israelites with regard to their civil affairs. Sure, the mosaic Law had some ceremonial and religious parts. But the law against domestic usury was to be administered in conjunction with their civil affairs. Dr. Brat's brain has not even begun to search out the depths of wisdom and knowledge found in the pages of the Bible. These laws formed a constitution in Ancient Israel for an entire nation, not small religious communities.

In *Part I* of this essay, we observed two opinions on usury, one from a jurist (Howard Rand) and one from a historian

(Michael Hoffman). Both are in agreement through analysis of all pertinent Scriptures. In Endnote [13] at the end of this *Part II* we have included the entirety of Leviticus Chapter 25. It behooves readers to learn this entire Bible chapter as the best basis we have for the prohibition against usury Jesus gave in Luke 6:35. Four additional Old Testament passages are also essential elements for this opinion. They are Psalm 15:1-5, Ezekiel 18:5, 8-9 and Ezekiel 22:12. The Lord Himself confirmed all four Bible passages with His Luke 6:35 statement. At the mouth of two or three witnesses the matter shall be established. Here we have five. How much more should we take heed of the Lord's admonition?

Furthermore, Dr. Brat has obviously never considered how oppressive student loans and mortgages can be on family life. Perhaps he should begin accumulating statistics on these two items so he can produce something worthwhile like the centerfold this writer produced in *Part I* of this essay on pages 28 and 29.

Look carefully at the following Line from Leviticus 25: *"And you shall consecrate the fiftieth year, and proclaim liberty throughout all the land to all its inhabitants. It shall be a Jubilee for you; and each of you shall return to his possession, and each of you shall return to his family."* This passage clearly states that everyone shall return to his possession. Did this not include the strangers living within the borders of greater Israel who also kept the law of the Lord? As Michael Hoffman pointed out in his *Usury in Christendom*, there were two types of strangers Biblically named, *ger* and *nokri*. They are two different classifications of aliens. One lived within Israel's borders permanently ; they kept Israel's divinely given laws. The other was the foreigner who was just passing through such as a merchant or a traveller. Israelites were only allowed to charge interest on loans of money to the foreigners such as merchants and travellers who did not reside in greater Israel, not to the resident aliens. Many illuminated Bible scholars would agree with this writer that all domestic usury was prohibited in ancient Israel's constitution. And this domestic usury also was not to be levied on resident aliens. What is the Bible's terminology for resident alien? When reading the Bible, look for strangers within their gates when reading all of Leviticus and Deuteronomy.

All this is *prima facie* evidence of Dr. Brat's claiming to know the facts in the matter, while not having actually read all the relevant Bible passages for himself carefully as perhaps a seminary student of Calvinism should.

The entire matter on usury in Lev. 25 has its basis spelled out explicitly. The reason for the prohibition against domestic usury is *oppression*. What kind of *oppression* could possibly be caused by usury? The first thing that comes to mind is *economic oppression* as the prices of all goods and services eventually evolve to become out of reach for those who aren't mentally and/or physically equipped to participate in such a system. In 1949 CR Dickey wrote a Horace Greeley quote from 1872 in her **[Is Economic Ruin Inevitable?]** **[10]**, *"We have stricken the shackles from four million human beings and brought all laborers to a common level, not so much by the elevation of the former slaves as by practically reducing the whole working population, white and black, to a condition of serfdom. While boasting of our noble deeds, we are careful to conceal the ugly fact that by our iniquitous money system we have nationalized a system of oppression which, though more refined, is not less cruel than the old system of chattel slavery."*

In the second part of this list Dr. Brat wrote the following: *"Money changers eventually began keeping deposits for various clients, so that when two clients made an exchange, all the money changers had to do was credit one account and subtract from the other. Simple arithmetic had replaced a risky and cumbersome movement of coins."* Here also we find his acknowledgment that the concept of credit was given life by the moneychangers. At first of course, when there were no certified public accountants to examine a moneychanger's account ledgers, an entirely new class of moneychanger emerged who was willing to cook his books any way he pleased. Jefferson pointed out to us, *"it is impossible to say at what point their notes will stop."* They only stop when the bankers think it's time to put the brakes on economic activity so they can confiscate some choice assets.

This is no doubt where the two column ledger was brought into existence in which the moneychanger began to be able to lend money that does not exist, and in effect create brand new money in every so called simple loan contract. Why doesn't Dr. Brat explain this?

On page 177 Dr. Brat explains that, *"When banks charge interest on a loan.....they're charging for something. By lending money, for instance, the bank is foregoing other opportunities to use the money, and it is taking a risk in lending the money in the first place."* What he did here is paint an entirely falsified picture of the modern moneychanger's loan transactions. Falsified, you ask? In this study we already noticed that banks do not have money to lend as bank credit. They create new money with every loan contract. It is called bank credit. One hundred years ago, the MIT professor of economics and statistics, Dewey, wrote that it was known as book credit during the Civil War. Dr. Brat should have explained that the moneychanger is not under the same risks as the borrower. He should even say that the moneychanger's risk factor is next to nothing compared to the borrower because either way the loan contract finishes the moneychanger wins - with collected fees up front, perhaps twenty years of collecting loan payments and possibly even confiscating the collateral in the event of a default. And who has control of when and where the bust cycles will occur in which the borrowers will lose their jobs as the result of layoffs? Who restricts credit to slow down or even stop robust economic activity? Certainly not borrowers!

There are two columns on the moneychangers' ledger. At the top of one column there is the word debit. The other column has the heading credit. People who have a credit card in their wallet use the credit column of the moneychangers' ledger regularly. They go to a store and swipe their cards to make purchases. There are usually fees and interest rates associated with the use of this card. The key feature is that the amount of any purchase made is electronically transmitted to the moneychanger's ledger (in cyberspace) into both columns. The debit column shows the same amount as the credit column. This entry in the debit column is the amount for which the moneychanger is liable. That's why they call the debit column liabilities. The credit column contains the moneylenders' assets. The credit amount is the borrower's responsibility to pay back to the moneychanger at interest. The principal amount that is paid back thus erases both entries that were initially entered when the card was swiped. But the moneychanger keeps the interest and fees that were paid by the borrower. This is a brief description of the wordplay bankers use to describe the process. We can easily describe it as, "abracadabra" – the power of illusion.

If debt/usury capitalism is so good, how is it that Dr. Brat missed the word 'mammon' in his Bible study? On page four of his *Usury in Christendom: The Mortal Sin that was and Now is Not*, Michael Hoffman offers this as his first Bible quotation of Christ's own words that were written in Matthew 6:24. It clearly indicates that one cannot be both a Christian and a modern economist according to Dr. Brat's definition of an economist.

With the verse containing the word mammon, we also include here Hoffman's commentary for the word. " *'No man can serve two masters, for either he will hate the one, and love the other ; or else he will hold to the one, and despise the other. Ye cannot serve God and mammon'. Mammon is derived from the Aramaic word for riches (mammon) occurring in the Greek text of Matthew vi. 24 and Luke xvi. 9-13, and retained in the Vulgate. Owing to the quasi-personification in these passages, the word was taken by mediaeval writers as the proper name of the devil of covetousness....From the 16th century onwards it has been current in English, usually with more or less of personification, as a term of opprobrium for wealth regarded as an idol or as an evil influence."* (Oxford English Dictionary).* So Dr. Brat, the Scriptures have thus condemned modern economists from entrance into the kingdom of heaven for choosing worldly economics over Biblical economics. There appears to be only one way for you to gain entrance. You really need to begin at square one and search for a better definition of economist that would nullify what you wrote in the fourth quotation of yours that was cited on page 88.

The Preamble Compared with
Ancient Israel's Constitution

In *Part I* we noted two modern scholars who demonstrated that both historical analysis and the Bible teach us the possibility exists that all mankind could benefit if God's laws would be observed. It would, of course, be very simple to administer such a system nationally. We have before us our American Constitution and ancient Israel's constitution as written in the Pentateuch or Torah. Careful examination of the Preamble reveals that if we carefully observed the objectives listed therein, we would also be in strict compliance with the laws listed in the Pentateuch.

The jurist Howard Rand, whose opinion was cited on usury in *Part I*, has perhaps written between twenty and thirty volumes himself. From a brief essay he wrote some years back called *From the Cradle to the Grave*, we should take note of his opinion on what the Preamble actually means to us as a basis for our system of laws. "We the people of the United States, in order to form a more perfect union, establish justice, insure domestic tranquility, provide for the common defense, promote the general welfare and secure the blessings of liberty to ourselves and our posterity, do ordain and establish this constitution for the United States of America." H.B. Rand lists the following five items from it that must be weighed with every action initiated by government for that action to be in compliance with the constitution:

"1) Establish justice.

2) Insure domestic tranquility.

3) Provide for the common defense.

4) Promote the general welfare.

5) Secure the blessings of liberty.

"Let us examine this list carefully, for the solution of human problems does not lie in changing the original purpose for which governments came into being, a purpose sanctioned by God, nor in changing or discounting the reasons for the writing of the Constitution of the United States, but in a restoration of the administration of laws that already exist, the keeping of which will assure the blessings of all these five points and more also – even freedom from want. We challenge those who propose to set up a form of government that will make everyone conscious of government in his

business, domestic and private life and that, instead of thus attaining their desired end (that is, tranquility and peace), will but establish inequalities, injustice, tyranny and oppression.

"Fundamental to righteous government is the establishment of justice."

This justice will never be accomplished with an unrighteous monetary system in operation as we now have. It has already been revealed in the Pentateuch, the Psalms, Ezekiel, the Lord Jesus Himself and one thousand five hundred years of Church history that the charging of interest on loans of money is not allowable. Michael Hoffman did not miss any of the Biblical and Church history interdictions against usury in his ***Usury in Christendom*** [9]. Also, during the past three hundred and twenty years, many different historical narratives show us clearly that a usurious monetary system is a bane upon civilization. Money and credit created out of nothing that is lent at interest is indeed a tool for economic oppression. Without attending to this severe problem with the outlawing of usury first (as Howard Rand put it), none of the objectives named in the Preamble will ever be attainable because the political class has evolved into a swarm of swindlers and shavers just like the bankers that Jefferson so named.

Most reformers today though, have not yet embraced the only vision that will overturn the beast of usury capitalism. They write about reform, but only a reform that has already been tried during Colonial America by followers of Franklin's philosophy [3] that moderate usury is not harmful. And still today, none suggest that bankers be stripped of their authority to create money as Jefferson did. Although some of the reform peddlers are very professional at articulating their cases, all will fall short of bringing in prosperity for the people. St. Paul wrote twice in his epistles, "A little leaven, leavens the whole lump." It doesn't take rocket science to demonstrate that as long as everyone can charge interest on loans of money, that interest always shows up in prices. Jefferson explained this very carefully with his observations on the price for a bushel of wheat. How did he miss that the interest charged by the Bank of the United States on the 'bills of credit' it issued as loans to the people would also wind up in the price of a bushel of wheat?

With this in mind then, we should analyze a couple of the plans modern reformers are now attempting to sell us. Very recently an email came to my inbox from a friend with whom I worked some 13 years ago. His name is Jim Owens. He, like me, is paying close attention to American politics. In that email he

Jim Owens – Christian Monetary Reformer

concerned himself with signing an electronic petition in support of Elizabeth Warren's most recent Postal Bank Proposal initiative at the following link:
https://www.credomobilize.com/petitions/sign-the-petition-allow-post-offices-to-offer-basic-banking-services-1?sp_ref=45558556.4.8014.e.0.2&source=mailto_sp%20.

U.S. Senator Elizabeth Warren of Massachusetts [14], like the attorney Ellen Brown from California, is promoting her own Public Bank Solution. That first sentence beginning Jefferson's quotation on Ford's page 392 Volume IX (see page 62) should make all of us want to run away from anything Ms. Brown and

US Senator Elizabeth Warren propose. Does either of them campaign to prohibit private banks from issuing currency and credit? Like Jefferson, neither would cut off the head of the beast. Neither would do away with usury. Neither would do away with private money creation. Neither would prohibit banks

US Senator Elizabeth Warren

Public Bank Advocate
Attorney Ellen Brown

Senator Warren's Promotion Advertisement

from injecting their bank credit into our money supply. Neither offers the alternatives needed to put down the grip the money power has upon civilization. For all the great analysis Jefferson wrote for us, he too suggested only one third of the solution needed to lead us out of money power control.

In Senator Warren's case, the US Postal Service would take on a dual role as both Bank and Post Office. But if our government became the only issuer of our currency, it could easily create all our money both to pay for the cost of government and to issue interest free loans to the people. To create our money supply in any other way opens the door for swindlers and shavers to prey on the people. Jefferson had already shown that the scenario Brown and Warren now propose ended in disaster for the people during his lifetime even with the First Bank of the United States issuing credit and legal tender. As we can easily see now, they did nothing to stop private banks from issuing their own notes and credit simultaneously.

This email Warren just recently sent out is a petition asking for signatures so she can see how many are interested in setting up the United States Postal Service with a public banking division in our local postal buildings. No doubt, it will be as Ellen Brown proposes: a public usury banking operation. It does seem there is no end to how many times people will choose the same disaster over and over leaving bankers to wreak havoc by creating our money and credit.

Multiple Currencies

But even worse than the simple, obvious analysis of what is in the last of Jefferson quotes from Ford's Volume IX pages 414, 415 (see pages 75,76) there are very undesirable conditions that prevail when multiple currencies are in operation. Early in America's history even foreign bank notes were allowed to circulate, Jefferson noted. Moreover, he explained very well what he witnessed with multiple currencies while he lived. Those who have it in mind to decentralize currencies set the stage for swindlers and shavers to operate much more easily as Jefferson's analysis demonstrates here, *"the only resource which the government could command with certainty, the States have unfortunately fooled away, nay corruptly alienated to swindlers and shavers, under the cover of private banks"*. At this point we should recall from page 30 in **Part I** precisely why Abraham Lincoln's treasury secretary Salmon P. Chase was in favor of instituting a national currency, *"uniformity of circulation, in place of a bank-note circulation dependent on the laws of 34 States and 1600 private corporations."* There are reformers active today who claim that decentralization is the key to keeping commercial systems free of predatory, monopoly banking. But the history Jefferson and Chase show here refutes that theory squarely. It is too bad that neither ever came to realize that usury is the real root of the problem.

An email came to my inbox by such a reformer recently who was a participant in Anthony Migchels' International Webinar Monetary Conference in April of 2014. On Apr 29, 2014, at 10:14 PM, Wayne Walton wrote: "Decentralized modern tribalism isn't anarchy. It's government based upon the NAP and local self-sufficiency. It's what occurs naturally without Monopoly money." So Mr. Walton has a theory. Does he suppose that natural law will prevail where money is involved as the von Mises advocates teach? Is not the natural law of human nature "the love of money"? Has he considered that the entire history of monetary practice has always been rooted in local creation of money as in book credit and local bank notes? Book credit is operating even now at the local level in private corporations called banks. Were conditions better in Jefferson's time with the absence of monopoly money? From Jefferson's writings we learn that conditions were just as bad when he lived or even worse. So Walton's desire for decentralized control is nothing new, and will again play out in one disaster after another, not as he envisions, because money is involved. Laws need to be established in order to prevent evildoers from plying their tradecraft. If this is not done nationally and uniformly, then we should expect exactly the same things to happen over and over again as it always has because there is no morality in practicing usury on simple loan contracts. Abolish usury so the effects of monopoly are nullified while only creating money to pay for government services and public infrastructure and thus establish a money supply. We should note that interest free credit is not a part of the permanent money supply. It disappears from the currency stream when it is paid back to the National Credit Agency. Since interest is not a factor in such a loan, it is not deflationary ; and new real wealth is created as the result of this practice of lending interest free.

Anti-Usury Dutch Economist Anthony Migchels [15]

A decentralized monetary system in which multiple local currencies are allowed by law will always wind up as anarchy, contrary to what Mr. Walton thinks. Jefferson's letters to Eppes spell out very carefully what happened when currencies were localized because two hundred years ago local bank notes weren't even uniform in the states. This anarchy sets up the unsophisticated for the con-artist ploys. The more the merrier, the scammers say, because when they open up their briefcases with an entire array of portfolios, they will have available even more garbage with which to pilfer from the honest earners. Perhaps Mr. Walton is one of those financial advisors who prey on those who do honest labor? The problems from Mr. Walton's ideas always become manifest whenever usury is used in simple loan contracts. What were Jefferson's words? *"the only resource which the government could command with certainty, the States have unfortunately fooled away, nay corruptly alienated to swindlers and shavers, under the cover of private banks.*" This assuredly will be the final outcome in Mr. Walton's system. Why? Will builders, contractors, tradespeople, doctors, lawyers and so on care to be paid in some local currency which they cannot carry to their next job that just happens to be in another region that refuses to accept the local currency they were paid with? Or what percentage will be necessary to pay for converting the hard earned money into a different regional or local currency?

We shall here take a little more space to enumerate some of the more disturbing conditions that prevail today. We shall see if Dr. David Brat's assessment of Adam Smith's and Alisa Rosenbaum's (Ayn Rand's) systems are worth any consideration.

There are homeless people living in cardboard boxes under freeway overpasses and in abandoned automobiles. If they had a job and a house previously, but lost the house through a tax foreclosure after getting laid off, it's because the present system requires property taxes. Even the jurist Howard Rand railed against confiscatory property taxes. There was no property tax in the Mosaic Law, nor does there need to be here in America in a non-usury based monetary system.

There are policemen and firemen unable to pay for medications for their families. We see crumbling highway infrastructure. We see local and state governments unable to adequately fund services. We see the constant clamor to privatize any advances in human services like Social Security for which the people have the right to collect its benefits after paying in a percentage of their earnings all their livelong days. Even military veterans who gave up almost everything serving their nation have trouble getting medical services. The people who work are taxed into oblivion to pay for all those who refuse to work, in addition to the criminals and those who through no fault of their own are

unable to work. The people who work must pay for it all. While
the wealthy are allowed loopholes in the tax structure so that they
do not pay their proportionate share of the burden.

Usury free levels the playing field. No national debt
means the costs of government, human services, and
infrastructure will all be all fully funded without fear of
overspending. The only loss would be that usurers might need to
learn a useful trade or profession to pay their way, rather than live
parasitically off of the usefulness of others. As a final word, we
shall again take note, that without usury, and with a federal
institution creating all our currency and credit, the only tax
necessary is a flat rate increase tax on incomes over an income
threshold for living expenses.

Conclusion

Thomas Jefferson was very industrious and brilliant, as
was Benjamin Franklin. Their accomplishments in the
Unanimous Declaration of Independence and Preamble paved a
substantial road for followers to incorporate the Bill of Rights as a
natural result of the two above-mentioned documents. But both
men had human foibles, as we all do. Both grew up in times when
the merchants of the world were preaching usury mercantilism as
a good thing. This was during Adam Smith's time. Jefferson
read Smith's work *The Wealth of Nations*. His mention of Smith
several times in his letters supports this. But for them, the time
had not yet arrived to grasp how great a magnet the love of money
really is in human nature. To them, moderate usury was actually
harmless. But as human beings, they were definitely not
omniscient and could not predict all the possible outcomes that
would eventually take shape in a debt/usury based capitalist
monetary system. Thus this one great *faux pas*, that would
undermine all the good they accomplished, was allowed into what
otherwise could have been a summit of human achievement.

Had they a little more faith that Jesus spoke as almighty

God, perhaps they would also have believed His interdiction against usury is based on His hatred of oppression along with His ability to predict human actions in a debt/usury based monetary system. This is a key feature of Leviticus 25 where all domestic usury is prohibited in conjunction with His command not to oppress the people.

Go to the Sermon on the Mount. Read all the sayings with 'blessed are they', the beatitudes. Instead of reading it 'blessed are they', read it is as 'blessed is Jesus' instead. He there told us about his own nature. "Blessed is Jesus who is meek ; who is pure in heart ; who hungers and thirsts after righteousness ; who is merciful ; who is a peacemaker ; who is persecuted for righteousness sake ; whom men revile and persecute. The Father seeks such people to serve Him.

This Jesus now sits at the right hand of the Father ; and the simplest of His instructions are summarily ignored by all the great ones on the earth. It is also written, "That which is highly esteemed among men is abomination in the eyes of God." All the lawyers, bankers and politicians are leading us on a path to destruction. Three hundred and twenty years have passed since the Bank of England was founded, and we have not yet conquered the love of money. The Lord has meekly stayed out of our affairs because we have chosen to bypass the simplest of His instructions. Only when we threaten to destroy His earth will He intervene ; and only when we call upon Him to save us.

Endnotes

[1]
Ford: http://catalog.hathitrust.org/Record/000366341
Bergh: http://catalog.hathitrust.org/Record/006664320

104

[2]
http://babel.hathitrust.org/cgi/pt?id=nyp.33433034399281;view=1up;seq=11

[3]
The Writings of Thomas Jefferson, Vol. VII page 87, 1896 – by
Paul Leicester Ford
http://babel.hathitrust.org/cgi/pt?id=mdp.39015005705853;view=
1up;seq=9
"Father of American Philosophy"

*A Modest Enquiry into the Nature and Necessity of a Paper-
Currency* by Benjamin Franklin, 1729
http://etext.lib.virginia.edu/users/brock/webdoc6.html

[4]
Money Creators by Gertrude Coogan, 1935.
Hidden Mysteries – TGS Publishers, 22241 Pinedale Lane,
Frankston, Texas 75763. *Money Creators* 2006. (903) 876 3256
www.hiddenmysteries.com
info@hiddenmysteries.com

[5]
The Writings of Thomas Jefferson, Vol. IX, 1898 by Paul
Leicester Ford
http://babel.hathitrust.org/cgi/pt?id=uc2.ark:/13960/t6833nn2f;vie
w=1up;seq=9

[6]
From a 2009 book with the title *Hoodwinked* by John Perkins (an
economist) on page 117 we can learn an understandable definition
of the financial term derivative: **"We have become a paper
economy, vulnerable to the whims of lawyers and investment**

bankers. The trading of corporations through mergers and acquisitions and the pushing of financial paper in the form of forwards, options, futures, swaps and other derivatives are huge parts of our system. When the economy peaked, just before the recession began in 2007, over 40 percent of U.S. profits were earned by the financial sector (although it turned out to be 'paper' profits). The very nature of a derivative – a financial contract which value depends on (is derived from) the value of something else (for example, a commodity, stock, home mortgage, market index) – belies the trust conveyed by paper. Perhaps it is a sign of the times that today paper pushers seldom use paper; they do it all with the push of a button, electronically."

[7]
During the 1930s a catholic pastor in Royal Oak, Michigan conducted a weekly radio broadcast that had an estimated forty-five million listeners. At least two of his broadcasts stand out as rants against the capitalist bankers. These titles were *Twenty Years Ago Today* and *Relief That Fails to Relieve*.
https://www.youtube.com/results?search_query=father+charles+coughlin

[8]
The Writings of Thomas Jefferson Volume VII page 31. 1896 - by Paul Leicester Ford, "Colossus of Federalism"
http://babel.hathitrust.org/cgi/pt?id=mdp.39015005705853;view=1up;seq=9

[9]
Usury in Christendom: The Mortal Sin that Was and Now is Not by Michael Hoffman, 2013.
http://revisionisthistorystore.blogspot.com/2010/03/michael-hoffmans-online-revisionist.html

[10]
http://www.destinypublishers.com

[11]
http://en.wikipedia.org/wiki/Emergency_Banking_Act

[12]
Financial History of the United States by Davis Rich Dewey, Ph.D, LL.D., 1915 – Professor of Economics and Statistics – Massachusetts Institute of Technology
http://books.google.com/books/about/Financial_History_of_the_United_States.html?id=l3oaAAAAMAAJ

[12] Continued
Banking in United States Before Civil War Vol. I
The first and second banks of the United States by John Thom Holdworth and Davis Rich Dewey, 1911. This one is also available for viewing on line at Google Books.
http://books.google.com/books?id=PSYiAQAAIAAJ&printsec=frontcover&source=gbs_ge_summary_r&cad=0#v=onepage&q&f=false

[13]
Leviticus Chapter 25 NKJV
The Sabbath of the Seventh Year
25 "And the Lord spoke to Moses on Mount Sinai, saying, **2** "Speak to the children of Israel, and say to them: 'When you come into the land which I give you, then the land shall keep a sabbath to the Lord. **3** Six years you shall sow your field, and six years you shall prune your vineyard, and gather its fruit; **4** but in the seventh year there shall be a sabbath of solemn rest for the land, a sabbath to the Lord. You shall neither sow your field nor prune your vineyard. **5** What grows of its own accord of your harvest you shall not reap, nor gather the grapes of your untended

vine, for it is a year of rest for the land. **6** And the sabbath produce of the land shall be food for you: for you, your male and female servants, your hired man, and the stranger who dwells with you, **7** for your livestock and the beasts that are in your land—all its produce shall be for food.

The Year of Jubilee

8 'And you shall count seven sabbaths of years for yourself, seven times seven years; and the time of the seven sabbaths of years shall be to you forty-nine years. **9** Then you shall cause the trumpet of the Jubilee to sound on the tenth day of the seventh month; on the Day of Atonement you shall make the trumpet to sound throughout all your land. **10** And you shall consecrate the fiftieth year, and proclaim liberty throughout all the land to all its inhabitants. It shall be a Jubilee for you; and each of you shall return to his possession, and each of you shall return to his family. **11** That fiftieth year shall be a Jubilee to you; in it you shall neither sow nor reap what grows of its own accord, nor gather the grapes of your untended vine. **12** For it is the Jubilee; it shall be holy to you; you shall eat its produce from the field.

13 'In this Year of Jubilee, each of you shall return to his possession. **14** And if you sell anything to your neighbor or buy from your neighbor's hand, you shall not oppress one another. **15** According to the number of years after the Jubilee you shall buy from your neighbor, and according to the number of years of crops he shall sell to you. **16** According to the multitude of years you shall increase its price, and according to the fewer number of years you shall diminish its price; for he sells to you according to the number of the years of the crops. **17** Therefore you shall not oppress one another, but you shall fear your God; for I am the Lord your God.

Provisions for the Seventh Year

18 'So you shall observe My statutes and keep My judgments, and perform them; and you will dwell in the land in safety. **19** Then the land will yield its fruit, and you will eat your fill, and dwell there in safety.

20 'And if you say, "What shall we eat in the seventh year, since we shall not sow nor gather in our produce?" **21** Then I will command My blessing on you in the sixth year, and it will bring forth produce enough for three years. **22** And you shall sow in the eighth year, and eat old produce until the ninth year; until its produce comes in, you shall eat of the old harvest.

Redemption of Property
23 'The land shall not be sold permanently, for the land is Mine; for you are strangers and sojourners with Me. **24** And in all the land of your possession you shall grant redemption of the land.

25 'If one of your brethren becomes poor, and has sold some of his possession, and if his redeeming relative comes to redeem it, then he may redeem what his brother sold. **26** Or if the man has no one to redeem it, but he himself becomes able to redeem it, **27** then let him count the years since its sale, and restore the remainder to the man to whom he sold it, that he may return to his possession. **28** But if he is not able to have it restored to himself, then what was sold shall remain in the hand of him who bought it until the Year of Jubilee; and in the Jubilee it shall be released, and he shall return to his possession.

29 'If a man sells a house in a walled city, then he may redeem it within a whole year after it is sold; within a full year he may redeem it. **30** But if it is not redeemed within the space of a full year, then the house in the walled city shall belong permanently to him who bought it, throughout his generations. It shall not be released in the Jubilee. **31** However the houses of villages which have no wall around them shall be counted as the fields of the country. They may be redeemed, and they shall be released in the

Jubilee. **32** Nevertheless the cities of the Levites, and the houses in the cities of their possession, the Levites may redeem at any time. **33** And if a man purchases a house from the Levites, then the house that was sold in the city of his possession shall be released in the Jubilee; for the houses in the cities of the Levites are their possession among the children of Israel. **34** But the field of the common-land of their cities may not be sold, for it is their perpetual possession.

Lending to the Poor
35 'If one of your brethren becomes poor, and falls into poverty among you, then you shall help him, like a stranger or a sojourner, that he may live with you. **36** Take no usury or interest from him; but fear your God, that your brother may live with you. **37** You shall not lend him your money for usury, nor lend him your food at a profit. **38** I am the Lord your God, who brought you out of the land of Egypt, to give you the land of Canaan and to be your God.

The Law Concerning Slavery
39 'And if one of your brethren who dwells by you becomes poor, and sells himself to you, you shall not compel him to serve as a slave. **40** As a hired servant and a sojourner he shall be with you, and shall serve you until the Year of Jubilee. **41** And then he shall depart from you—he and his children with him—and shall return to his own family. He shall return to the possession of his fathers. **42** For they are My servants, whom I brought out of the land of Egypt; they shall not be sold as slaves. **43** You shall not rule over him with rigor, but you shall fear your God. **44** And as for your male and female slaves whom you may have—from the nations that are around you, from them you may buy male and female slaves. **45** Moreover you may buy the children of the strangers who dwell among you, and their families who are with you, which they beget in your land; and they shall become your property. **46** And you may take them as an inheritance for your children

110

after you, to inherit them as a possession; they shall be your permanent slaves. But regarding your brethren, the children of Israel, you shall not rule over one another with rigor.

47 'Now if a sojourner or stranger close to you becomes rich, and one of your brethren who dwells by him becomes poor, and sells himself to the stranger or sojourner close to you, or to a member of the stranger's family, 48 after he is sold he may be redeemed again. One of his brothers may redeem him; 49 or his uncle or his uncle's son may redeem him; or anyone who is near of kin to him in his family may redeem him; or if he is able he may redeem himself. 50 Thus he shall reckon with him who bought him: The price of his release shall be according to the number of years, from the year that he was sold to him until the Year of Jubilee; it shall be according to the time of a hired servant for him. 51 If there are still many years remaining, according to them he shall repay the price of his redemption from the money with which he was bought. 52 And if there remain but a few years until the Year of Jubilee, then he shall reckon with him, and according to his years he shall repay him the price of his redemption. 53 He shall be with him as a yearly hired servant, and he shall not rule with rigor over him in your sight. 54 And if he is not redeemed in these years, then he shall be released in the Year of Jubilee—he and his children with him. 55 For the children of Israel are servants to Me; they are My servants whom I brought out of the land of Egypt: I am the Lord your God."

[14]
http://en.wikipedia.org/wiki/Elizabeth_Warren

[15]
Anthony Migchels is an economist who lives in Netherlands. His blogs are posted regularly at realcurrencies.wordpress.com

One of his most recent on derivatives is enlightening and factual.
Use the following url to access it for reading:
http://realcurrencies.wordpress.com/2014/06/15/derivatives-or-
how-the-money-power-created-the-greatest-depression/

CPSIA information can be obtained
at www.ICGtesting.com
Printed in the USA
FSOW02n0723121114
3445FS